The Russian Budget

The Russian budget process has received little detailed attention in academic literature. Here various key aspects of the formation of the federal budget, largely since Vladimir Putin began his third presidential term in 2012, are examined. It is primarily the writing of the expenditure side of the budget which is described, that is, how it is decided how much money is spent on what. While ample information is provided on budgetary outcomes, the focus is on the process: the issues faced by budget makers, the actors and institutions involved, and the formal and informal procedures that lead to outcomes. It is not the task of the volume to provide an analysis of the wisdom or effectiveness of particular budget allocations; its goal is to provide some judgement on the effectiveness of the process. Chapters are offered on the budgetary process as it relates to the two main claimants on federal budget funding, the social and defence sectors. Three chapters then examine the major locations of budgetary policy-making: the executive (at presidential and cabinet of ministers levels), the Duma, and the expert community.

This book was originally published as a special issue of *Post-Communist Economies.*

Stephen Fortescue is an Honorary Associate Professor at the University of New South Wales, Australia, and a Visiting Fellow in the Centre for European Studies at the Australian National University. He is a specialist on the Russian policy-making process, particularly as it relates to economic policy.

The Russian Budget

Edited by
Stephen Fortescue

Routledge
Taylor & Francis Group
LONDON AND NEW YORK

First published 2019
by Routledge
2 Park Square, Milton Park, Abingdon, Oxon, OX14 4RN, UK

and by Routledge
52 Vanderbilt Avenue, New York, NY 10017

First issued in paperback 2020

Routledge is an imprint of the Taylor & Francis Group, an informa business

British Library Cataloguing in Publication Data
A catalogue record for this book is available from the British Library

ISBN 13: 978-0-367-58374-3 (pbk)
ISBN 13: 978-1-138-32272-1 (hbk)

Typeset in Myriad Pro
by RefineCatch Limited, Bungay, Suffolk

Publisher's Note
The publisher accepts responsibility for any inconsistencies that may have arisen during the conversion of this book from journal articles to book chapters, namely the possible inclusion of journal terminology.

Contents

Citation Information

The chapters in this book were originally published in *Post-Communist Economies*, volume 29, issue 4 (December 2017). When citing this material, please use the original page numbering for each article, as follows:

Chapter 1
Russian federal budget formation: introduction
Stephen Fortescue
Post-Communist Economies, volume 29, issue 4 (December 2017), pp. 449–456

Chapter 2
The social budget policy process in Russia at a time of crisis
Marina Khmelnitskaya
Post-Communist Economies, volume 29, issue 4 (December 2017), pp. 457–475

Chapter 3
The Russian budgetary process and defence: finding the 'golden mean'
Julian Cooper
Post-Communist Economies, volume 29, issue 4 (December 2017), pp. 476–490

Chapter 4
Russian experts: missing actors of the budget process
Lev Jakobson
Post-Communist Economies, volume 29, issue 4 (December 2017), pp. 491–504

Chapter 5
Amending budget bills in the Russian State Duma
Ben Noble
Post-Communist Economies, volume 29, issue 4 (December 2017), pp. 505–522

Chapter 6
The role of the executive in Russian budget formation
Stephen Fortescue
Post-Communist Economies, volume 29, issue 4 (December 2017), pp. 523–537

Notes on Contributors

Julian Cooper is Professor Emeritus at the Centre for Russian and East European Studies, the University of Birmingham, UK. He is also an Associate Senior Fellow with the Stockholm International Peace Research Institutes, Stockholm, Sweden.

Stephen Fortescue is an Honorary Associate Professor at the University of New South Wales, Australia, and a Visiting Fellow at the Centre for European Studies at the Australian National University.

Lev Jakobson is First Vice Rector and Professor in the Faculty of Economic Sciences/ Department of Applied Economics at the National Research University Higher School of Economics, Laboratory for Nonprofit Sector Studies at the Center for Studies of Civil Society and the Nonprofit Sector, Moscow, Russian Federation.

Marina Khmelnitskaya is a Post-Doctoral Researcher at the Centre of Excellence in Russian Studies, Aleksanteri Institute, University of Helsinki, Finland.

Ben Noble is a Lecturer in Russian Politics at the School of Slavonic and East European Studies, University College London, UK. He is also a Senior Research Fellow at the Higher School of Economics, Moscow, Russia, in the Laboratory for Regional Political Studies.

INTRODUCTION

Russian federal budget formation: introduction

Stephen Fortescue

The articles in this special issue describe various aspects of the formation of the federal budget in Russia today, largely since Vladimir Putin began his third presidential term in 2012. It is above all the writing of the expenditure side of the budget which is described, expenditures which in 2015 made up 19.33% of GDP (Ministerstvo Finansov RF, 2016; gks.ru/free_doc/new_site/vvp/vvp-god/Tab1.htm).

The budget process does not deal with the revenue side, except in the early stages when revenues are estimated by the Ministry of Finance (MF) on the basis of broad economic parameters forecast by the Ministry of Economic Development (MED). Confirmation of forecasts is highly contested, with MF and the Central Bank more often than not contesting MED's estimates. However, the actual raising of revenues – tax and other revenue-raising arrangements – is debated and determined in a separate process, with a different set of actors. Thus, the hydrocarbons sector – from which the greatest share of federal revenues is obtained – is barely represented in the budget process. That applies to the Ministry of Energy as well as to the major corporations in the sector. They are, however, at the heart of tax debates.

So the articles here are essentially about how it is decided how much money is spent on what. A serious effort has been made, within the limitations to be described below, to describe the process, not just the outcomes. It is not the task of the authors to provide an analysis of the wisdom or effectiveness of particular budget allocations; it is a goal to provide some judgement on the effectiveness of the process. In offering some comments on what I see as the picture to come out of the articles presented here, I note that what follows are my own views and reflect my particular interests, not necessarily those of the other authors represented here.

My own article opens by setting out the participants, process and procedures of the budgetary process within the executive. Formally, Russia's is a semi-presidential executive, meaning that a prime minister, not the president, chairs the cabinet. This means, given the undoubted pre-eminence of Putin in Russian policy-making, that a good part of the article is devoted to how and to what extent the president exerts his authority over a budget process which is largely centred operationally within government ministries and government councils and commissions. Ben Noble follows with an account of the parliament's involvement, and Lev Jakobson then analyses the involvement of experts. There are then two articles setting out how the two major recipients of budget revenues get their share of the pie: Marina Khmelnitskaya on social spending and Julian Cooper on the defence budget. As important as those two budget expenditure items are, to concentrate on them means that

Table 1. Russian federal budget expenditures, 2015, billion rubles.

Budget category	Amount
General state expenses	1117.6
Military (def)	3181.4
National security and law enforcement (def)	1965.6
National economy (dev)	2324.2
Housing services (soc)	144.1
Environment (soc)	49.7
Education (soc)	610.6
Culture and film (soc)	89.9
Health (soc)	516.0
Social policy (soc)	4265.3
Physical culture and sport (soc)	73.0
Mass media (soc)	82.1
Debt service	518.7
Inter-budget transfers (reg)	682.0
Total	15,620.3

Notes: (def) – budget categories usually included in the 'defence' sector; (dev) – budget category usually included in the 'development' sector; (soc) – budget categories usually included in the 'social' sector; (reg) – budget category usually included in the 'regional' sector. 'General state expenses' consists of expenditure on government administration at all levels.
Source: Ezhegodnaia informatsiia ob ispolnenii federal'nogo biudzheta (dannye s 1 ianvaria 2006 g.), 27 December 2016, minfin.ru/ru/statistics/fedbud/.

some important recipients are not considered. For example allocations from the federal budget to the regions took 4.37% of total federal expenditure in 2015.[1] This important aspect of the budget process has not been included partly for space reasons, but also because it is recognised that it has been well covered in other publications (Ermasova & Mikesell, 2016; Thiessen, 2006; Vartapetov, 2011). Also what could be very broadly called 'development' spending has no dedicated article, an omission to which I will return later in this Introduction.

By force of circumstance, the coverage is largely of the budget process as it is revealed in the public domain, and therefore largely as carried on by and between formal bodies and their representatives in formal or semi-formal forums. This is obviously a major limitation in the case of defence spending, for which not just much of the detail of budget allocations is secret, but also the process itself. More broadly important is the likelihood that much of the budget process even outside the defence budget, while not formally classified, is also carried on behind closed doors. Indeed the general picture of the Russian system we are presented with by commentators both academic and otherwise is that just about anything, and certainly anything important, goes on behind the scenes and probably in the form of informal interactions between people with close personal ties. The authors represented here are well aware of the methodological trap of assuming that the visible story is the whole story, and also recognise that recognising the trap is not the same as escaping it.

Open versus closed, formal versus informal, institutionalised versus personalist

The three binaries in the heading to this section by no means co-exist in a perfect symmetry of the first-mentioned versus the second-mentioned. Nevertheless it could be said that the second-mentioned form together the consensus view of the Russian system, that a relatively small elite, most members of which have some personal links with each other, rule in closed and informal ways. What institutions there are, operating openly and formally, exist at best as the instruments of a closed, personalist elite, and at worst as a complete facade. It would take a brave analyst to reject such a view; however I have long been of the view that the open, formal, institutionalised side of things is worthy of close attention, even if on no better grounds than it is unlikely that a complex, modern society such as Russia's can be run purely on the basis of the closed, informal and personalist (Fortescue, 2010a).

In the case of the budget process there is an extended and detailed formal process that can be followed in the public domain. It is a process which includes robust competition for budget allocations; it is one in which bureaucratic agencies, with their own in-house expertise but often assisted and informed by affiliated experts, pursue the interests of the sector of the economy or society for which they are responsible. Generally the positions and arguments of the participants are quite predictable and it could be said 'technocratic': those pursuing budget allocations do so because it is their job to do so, and they have the technical skills needed to make a convincing case, as well as access to the skills of experts. To some extent the outcomes are also predictable: if an outside observer has a reasonable idea of what have been identified as the needs of the society, reasonable predictions can be made as to whether and even to what extent they will be met through the budget process.

I am not, however, so naive as to leave it at that. It is true that there is a degree to which the 'objective' needs of society can be identified, and then one can trace a formal, institutionalised process that goes into action to meet those needs. A complex, modern society has to allocate some funding to its defence, its social security and its reproduction, and it has to have some sort of technical process to determine what those allocations should be. But there is very considerable room for a 'subjective' or 'political' element in identifying and prioritising those needs. To what extent is that 'subjective' element observable in the institutionalised process described in the articles in this special issue? To a limited extent only, it has to be said.

The 'subjective' parameters within which the budget process operates are largely set elsewhere, as broad political goals. Some of the most important in the period covered here are the May decrees,[2] military modernisation and the substantial increases in the defence budget it has required, and arguably import substitution, although its full significance for the budget and the economy more broadly is yet to be fully determined. The first two, in particular, feature prominently in the analyses offered here. Another major political parameter, one that sets the boundaries for all the others, is Putin's quite consistent commitment to fiscal discipline.

These parameters do not exist purely as givens that have emerged from a black box in order to be then inserted into the budget process. There is some public element to their setting and debate over their desirability, and some of that debate is aired within or close to the budget process. Of the four major parameters mentioned in the previous paragraph, three – the social spending component of the May decrees, import substitution and fiscal discipline – are all widely debated in the public domain, in a way which is reflected in the budget process. Not surprisingly, defence spending is less discussed in the public domain, but is by no means absent, surfacing on occasion in the budget process itself, most famously by Aleksei Kudrin – long-standing Minister of Finance (2000–2011) – in a way that led eventually to his dismissal.

The debate over the parameters within the budget process is not irrelevant or insignificant, but large-scale decisions – that there will be, say, a significant boost to the salaries of state employees or to the modernisation of the armed forces – are taken elsewhere. Perhaps a concentrated effort to trace how such decisions are made would reveal a degree of institutionalisation of that process, but that is not undertaken here and one hesitates to predict the outcome of such a study. Even the precise circumstances of the taking of what could be called second-order decisions – for example, that pensions not be fully indexed or what growth rate should be 'forecast' in budgetary planning – are not revealed in the official record of institutional interaction on which we have little choice but to rely. However in those cases the decisions are sufficiently embedded in the budget process which we are able to follow, that we can be reasonably confident that we know who is involved and what arguments are put forward. We can also be confident that the final decisions, even in second-order cases, are made by Putin. It is quite possibly the case that he is reluctant to take such decisions himself, but the indications are that he is given no choice (Fortescue, 2016, pp. 444–446).

Might this picture – of a process which takes place within parameters set outside but which then, while not without its closed informal characteristics, is essentially one that can be followed in considerable detail through openly available accounts of the formal activities of bureaucratic agencies – be entirely misleading? Might there be an entire closed, informal and personalist element which is not accounted for here, and which might indeed be far more important in determining who gets what? Quite possibly there is, but particularly if we exclude standard informal smoothing of the formal process (the informal discussions between agency heads before a formal meeting to sort out things in advance) there is little evidence of informal lobbying within the budget process of such a scale that totally unexpected outcomes occur. Perhaps it is too narrowly technocratic a process for that. The ideas and interests of interested parties external to the process are hardwired into the positions of 'their' bureaucratic actors, whose task is to pursue those ideas and interests within a process expressly created for that purpose. The key lobbying, including plausibly of an informal and personalist kind, comes before the budget process gets underway. It is also not hard to believe that there is a lot of lobbying at the implementation stage.

The protagonists

The evidence of the articles here suggests that the debate and bargaining that makes up so much of the budget process is between MF and the other participants. A lot of it is between MF, as the chief protector of budget discipline, and MED, whose role is much harder to define. It is not a spending ministry, and therefore is not bidding for money. However traditionally it has pursued something of a pro-growth agenda based on infrastructure spending. That puts it at odds with MF not just in terms of how and how much money should be spent, but also in terms of its forecasts of economic conditions. It is inclined to offer forecasts which provide room for spending, something that brings a negative reaction from MF (and the Central Bank). The budget process also entails a great deal of difficult interaction between MF and the recipients of government expenditure. In terms of the articles here, the main recipients are the social block and the defence sector. As best we can tell from the public record, these funding recipients fight for their allocations with MF. Although they often do so in a collective forum, there is no sense that they openly compete with each other. We do not have a sufficiently full record of what goes on at such meetings to arrive at a confident conclusion, but it appears that the representatives of the social block do not criticise defence spending or point out how it could be cut to their benefit, and vice versa. The two sides make their bids to MF, and argue their own cases on their merits.

To put it that way is not to suggest that everything is ultimately decided by MF. Much of the process is after all carried on in collective bodies in which MF is just one participant. In a way which will be specified in more detail immediately below, most of those collective bodies are within the government and are chaired by the prime minister. As is well known, Dmitrii Medvedev has had his policy preferences in terms of how economic growth should be pursued and therefore presumably how funding should be allocated. He had some opportunity to realise those preferences as president in the years 2008–2012; it is much less obvious that he is able to do so as prime minister. All the evidence is that he acts almost entirely as Putin's mouthpiece, and with only limited effectiveness. He clearly struggles to force participants to agree on the most difficult issues, leaving the need for appeal to the higher authority. We know that deputy prime ministers and some key ministers have direct access to Putin (in both formal and informal meetings one-on-one and at meetings with broader participation). We do not have direct evidence that they use such meetings to pursue their own budget preferences, but it would be surprising if they did not.

So far I have spoken as if the broad spending blocs – social, defence, development – are homogenous entities with no internal divisions. That is clearly not the case. There are major divisions within each – 'productive' versus 'non-productive' social spending, purely military versus security and law enforcement spending, infrastructure versus industrial development spending. Then there are the obvious competing interests within even those broad categories. Again not surprisingly, how this competition is fought out within the defence budget is least transparent, and seemingly not at all in the budget process described here. In the case of the other sectors a range of budget process participants, not just those with direct responsibility for the particular sector, take positions on what forms of social and development spending should be given priority. It is less clear, though, that those participants are able to determine these matters, that MED, say, is able to insist that development spending go on infrastructure or MF that social spending go on 'productive' budget lines, even if those are their publicly stated budget preferences.

I stated above that most of the budget process takes place within the government, in the narrow Russian sense of that part of the executive that is supervised by the prime minister. I have already qualified that statement by noting that the president, despite operating within a semi-presidential system, has a fundamentally important role to play, in setting broad budget parameters and injecting himself when needed into the operational process. To a large extent the latter is done through direct contact between the president and government officials, both as individuals and in collective structures. But the presidential administration is also involved, although I would suggest – not with, it must be said, total confidence – in a relatively minor way. The same, it seems, can be said of a whole host of other bodies, some of which have received concentrated attention in the articles here and others barely mentioned. The parliament has a major formal role, as a legislature voting on the Budget Law, but as Noble suggests, even what appears to be parliamentary involvement is likely to be in fact an extension of the executive part of the budget process. (He does note that his analysis is of changes to the budget during its passage through the Duma, and he does not exclude the possibility of the influence of deputies on budget formation outside the parliamentary process, perhaps particularly in the preliminary stages.) Jakobson describes the activities of experts as individuals and in expert bodies, but comes to the conclusion that they are under- and mis-used on both the demand and supply side. The Security Council is worthy of special mention, since it is sometimes described as the Russian Politburo. But neither as a collective body (the regular meetings of the permanent members rather than the rarer meetings of the full membership) nor as a bureaucratic apparatus does it feature in the accounts of the budget process that we have access to. Cooper provides some useful evidence that the Security Council can be used at least as a place of appeal if the defence budget appears to be under threat. But particularly with regard to influence on the broader budget process I am prepared to stick to my principle – although again without total confidence – that lack of evidence of involvement probably means lack of involvement. Other bodies such as the Accounting Office, political parties, business associations, NGOs, the Popular Front and so on, receive little or no attention in the articles here. That is partly a matter of word limits, and they would no doubt be included to some degree in much more extensive accounts. But when authors are restricted by word limits, they make decisions as to what is more and less important, and I trust that the right decisions have been made in the case of these bodies.

The recipients

The two main recipients of budget expenditures in the special issue are the social sphere and the defence sector. As already noted, there is another general recipient (beyond the regions), what I have called 'development'. Its absence as the subject of an article of its own is not a reflection of my view of its lack of importance in the Russian political economy. There would have been such an article if my efforts to find an author had been more successful. Nevertheless, it is the case that development is seen as the poor cousin of budget allocations. Whether more money should be allocated to it has long been a matter of debate, a debate consistently lost by those proposing increased spending. In my view, that is because Putin has never been a firm supporter, plus the lack of natural supporters among the other participants in the budget process. Its major champion has been Medvedev, not something to inspire optimism; MED has not been much more effective in promoting such an agenda. That is something that might well be changing, as even Putin is forced to contemplate a possibly extended period of low growth rates. We see him stressing the importance of the defence industry as a 'locomotive' of growth and an urgently increased emphasis on import substitution following the imposition of sanctions. That might suggest an increased prominence in the budget process of the Ministry of Industry and Trade and its minister Denis Manturov. The development budget has not only a growth side to it, but also a perhaps contradictory social side, as 'industry policy' funding is used to support sunset industries and the one-company towns (*monogoroda*) in which they are situated. The uncertainty as to how these developments might influence the budget was summed up well when in November 2016 Putin met Maksim Oreshkin, the newly appointed Minister of Economic Development, replacing the arrested and dismissed Aleksei Uliukaev. Oreshkin's previous position was deputy Minister of Finance and before that head of MF's Department of Long-term Strategic Planning, after a career in banking. In a classic but cautious example of the importance of 'hats' in officials' behaviour (Fortescue, 2010b, pp. 11–15), Oreshkin, despite his background in MF, responded to Putin's question as to what he saw as the most important issue facing the Russian economy:

> The rate of growth is, of course, inadequate. The most important task for the following year is the preparation of key measures that would allow us to remove structural barriers to the growth of the Russian economy and allow it to move forward.

He was determinedly vague when Putin then asked how he hoped to achieve such growth (kremlin.ru/events/president/news/53363).

Conclusion

Russia is a complex, modern society with a technocratic culture. It has a budget process to match, which can be reasonably well understood by following a formal, institutionalised process. That is not to say that it operates in a bureaucratic sealed room. It operates within parameters set in other ways and other forums. There are also, no doubt, informal components of the budget process itself to which we do not have access. However they appear to be not of such salience, or not operating against the flow of the formal open process to the degree that things happen that make no sense or are complete surprises to us. The same cannot be said of many other aspects of Russian political life.

It is a reasonably efficient process within the parameters that are set for it. Albeit requiring ever later deadlines,[3] budgets are drawn up based on reasonable and even conservative forecasts, the priorities set by the president are more or less funded after extensive discussions and negotiations, and the outcomes – at least in terms of macroeconomic outcomes if not programme implementation – are economically acceptable. It is a process which has been able to cope reasonably well in conditions of crisis, both in 2008 and 2014. It might be argued that the reasonable efficiency is at least partly because the right balance in the way the process works has been found between the institutionalised and technically competent representation of ideas and interests and the personal intervention of a cautious and politically-aware president.

But might the process struggle if economic circumstances put the simultaneous achievement of all priorities under greater strain? There are some areas which appear to have become chronic problems, the solution of which is constantly put off: the budget difficulties of the regions, pensions and many would say basic infrastructure. What more might be added to that list if serious choices have to be made between guns and butter? Putin cannot rely on the budget process to make his difficult decisions for him, even if he constantly tries to get it to at least take off the sharp edges. He likes his role to consist of setting the big targets and then, if needed, settling marginal decisions on how they can all be met, usually in the form of a 'golden mean' solution.[4] Will that work if the golden mean cannot be found? There were signs of strain in the 2017–2019 budget round: tax issues becoming part of the process, with the hydrocarbon sector which is not well represented in the institutionalised budget process being targeted; harsher fights over forecasts and the continued insistence on what could well be unrealistic growth targets; the introduction of the 'project office' as yet another approach to enforcing priorities; the use of Rosneftegaz dividends as, in Putin's words, a 'reserve ... when the government forgets that there are priorities that have to receive attention' (Papchenkova & Vorob'ev, 2016); and even a seemingly small thing such as MF not circulating budget documents in advance of major meetings.

It is not clear – and I will not attempt to predict here – whether economic circumstances will continue to worsen to the degree that the budget process will be put under serious new strain, much less whether the process will cope with those strains. But it is hoped that the articles in this special issue help identify where the strengths and weaknesses are, and will assist those who wish or need to form an opinion on the robustness of the future capacity of the system to do so.

Notes

1. Some sense of the complexities of what expenditure items are included in what budget lines can be gained from the articles in this issue, although a dedicated article would be needed to do the issue justice. The official distribution for 2015 is shown in Table 1.
2. A series of presidential decrees signed by Putin soon after returning to the presidency in 2012, they prescribed the implementation of campaign promises he had made before the election in a number of newspaper articles.
3. See Noble in this issue.
4. See Cooper in this issue.

Disclosure statement

No potential conflict of interest was reported by the author.

References

Ermasova, N., & Mikesell, J. (2016). Fiscal disparity and equalisation in the Russian Federation. *Post-Communist Economies, 28*(1), 1–15.

Fortescue, S. (2010a). Institutionalization and personalism in the policy-making process of the Soviet Union and post-Soviet Russia. In Stephen Fortescue (Ed.), *Russian politics from Lenin to Putin* (pp. 21–50). Basingstoke: Palgrave.

Fortescue, S. (2010b). TH. Rigby on Soviet and post-Soviet Russian politics, In Stephen Fortescue (ed.), *Russian politics from Lenin to Putin* (pp. 1–20). Basingstoke: Palgrave.

Fortescue, S. (2016). Russia's 'Turn to the East': A study in policy making. *Post-Soviet Affairs, 32*, 423–454.

Ministerstvo Finansov RF. (2016). *Ezhegodnaia informatsiia ob ispolnenii federal'nogo biudzheta (dannye s 1 ianvaria 2006 g.)* [Annual information on the implementation of the federal budget (data from 1 January 2006)], 27 December. minfin.ru/ru/statistics/fedbud/

Papchenkova, M., & Vorob'ev, A. (2016). Vladimir Putin: 'Rosneftegaz' – eto eshche odin biudzhet pravitel'stva [Vladimir Putin: 'Rosneftegaz' - it's another budget for the government]. *Vedomosti*, 26 December.

Thiessen, U. (2006). Fiscal Federalism in Russia: Theory, Comparisons, Evaluations. *Post-Soviet Affairs, 22*, 189–224.

Vartapetov, K. (2011). Russian Fiscal Federalism under Stress: Federal Support of Regions during the Global Financial Crisis. *Eurasian Geography and Economics, 52*, 529–542.

The social budget policy process in Russia at a time of crisis

Marina Khmelnitskaya

ABSTRACT
This article examines the process of Russian social budget formation during 2015–2016, a period marked by a significant reduction in state revenues due to changes in Russia's economic and international environment. Participants in the budget process included the president, prime minister, the financial-economic and social blocs of government, and experts outside the government. An important concern associated with the social sphere was maintaining political popularity. Budget formation in this area occurred via bureaucratic bargaining, with the president intervening only on the most salient issues. Examples of policy elaboration including indexation of major benefits and the freezing of pension contributions are considered.

«Просто денег нет сейчас. Найдем деньги – сделаем индексацию. Вы держитесь здесь, вам всего доброго, хорошего настроения и здоровья».[1]

During his visit to Crimea in late May 2016, Prime Minister Dmitrii Medvedev, responding to a question about the indexation of pensions from a local pensioner, used the phrase cited in the epigraph above. Slightly modified from its original, the phrase 'Денег нет, но вы держитесь' became an instant classic, inviting creative responses among the users of Russian social media.[2] 'There is no money, but you hang in (there)' encapsulates a host of issues related to the financing of Russian government social obligations in conditions of a severe revenue shortfall. Following years of economic growth since the early 2000s, which brought budget expansions and rises in personal income interrupted only by the impact of the Global Financial Crisis (GFC), in the last two years Russian policy-makers have started making adjustments to a new economic reality. The crisis into which the Russian economy plummeted in the second half of 2014 arose chiefly from the twin shocks of the drop in oil prices and international sanctions in response to the Ukraine crisis, but was precipitated by the weakening of the Russian economy during a period of stagnant growth in 2012–2013 (World Bank, 2016).

The crisis hit Russian government finances as well as Russian households hard. According to Aleksei Kudrin, former finance minister who recently resumed an important policy-making role,[3] the fall in the oil price led to a 4% reduction in GDP.[4] This is equivalent to the entire education budget and more than the healthcare budget. In addition, average real incomes over the period 2014–2016 declined. In 2015 average household income dropped by 4.1%, and 5.6% in 2016. Average monthly real wages were 100.7% of their level a year earlier, whereas real pensions were 96.6% compared to 2015.[5] Official poverty levels increased from 11.2% in 2012 to 15.7% in the first half of 2016 (Burdyak & Grishina, 2016). In conditions of declining incomes and consumption, most Russians are reliant on state social support, in the form of pensions, welfare benefits and salaries of public sector employees (Maleva, 2016, p. 16). In an environment of reduced budget revenues, declines in real incomes and high expectations associated with state social provision make budget cuts in the social sphere a highly contentious issue.

Social policy is important for the Russian state in both ideological and monetary terms. It has occupied an important place in strategic documents – notably Concept 2020 (adopted in 2008) and Strategy 2020 (published in 2012) – and the May decrees of Vladimir Putin. In these documents social policy is seen as an integral component of Russia's pursuit of a greater role on the global stage, economic development and security (Connolly, 2013; Cooper, 2012). This emphasis is due to a number of factors: the realisation by policy-makers of Russia's extremely poor demographic outlook; the perception of the failings of the liberal social reforms introduced in the early 2000s; the growing developmental aspirations of the ruling elite; and electoral motives. All these factors have reinforced each other over the last decade to give special significance to social measures, leading the government to develop new policies and institutional structures in the social sphere. Even though over the last decade the growth of social spending was not out of proportion with the growth of consolidated budget expenditure as a whole (Sutela, 2012; see Table 1 below), nonetheless it constitutes the state's largest expense item. Over 60% of consolidated budget outlays are directed to four broad sub-fields: (1) housing and housing services; (2) education, culture and mass media; (3) health and sport; and (4) social security including pensions. In conditions of Russia's heightened international role, social spending has to be balanced with other significant budgetary items, particularly defence spending, the share of which in the 2016 federal budget is 24% (Visloguzov, 2016a).[6] Drawing on examples from different areas of social policy, this article concentrates on the two most contentious issues involving the social sphere in the crisis budget process: the indexation of the salaries of state sector employees (*biudzhetniki*) and social payments, specifically old-age pensions and Maternity Capital, the latter by far the largest social benefit with implications for Russian demographic and housing policies.

Table 1. Consolidated government budget* expenditures – social policy share of total expenditure, %.

	Social policy, total**	Housing and housing services	Education, culture and mass media	Health and sport	Social security, including pensions
2005	60.3	6.9	14.0	11.7	27.7
2006	61.8	7.5	14.6	11.5	28.2
2007	60.9	9.7	14.0	12.1	25.1
2008	59.6	8.1	13.9	10.9	26.6
2009	59.1	6.3	13.1	10.3	29.4
2010	63.6	6.1	12.8	9.7	35.1
2011	62.2	6.0	13.2	10.5	32.6
2012	61.7	4.6	13.0	10.7	33.4
2013	62.2	4.2	13.4	10.0	34.6
2014	58.5	3.6	12.9	10.1	31.9
2015	61.0	3.3	12.0	10.5	35.2
2016	60–60.5	3.2	11.7	10.9	about 34.5 ***

*Federal budget, regional and local budgets, and state social funds; **Sum of the four columns that follow; ***Preliminary data.; Source: Russian Ministry of Finance and BOFIT.

This article builds on the academic literature covering Vladimir Putin's leadership, combined with a thorough reading of official government and media sources for the period since late 2014. The foundation for the article's argument derives from the comparative political science and social policy literatures, their institutionalist strand specifically – what can be summarised as 'politics matters' in defining welfare arrangements (Cook, 2007). This scholarship argues that the impact of structural factors, such as the effects of drastic reductions in state budget revenues on welfare policy decisions, is mediated by the influence of political factors. Thus, the article focuses on the interrelated influence of policy actors' interests and expert ideas in the negotiation of reductions in social spending, in conditions of Russia's non-democratic political regime.

The analysis also follows 'institutionalist' as opposed to 'personality-based' explanations of the policy process in Russia (Fortescue, 2016, 2017; Remington, 2015). This literature argues that the institutional structure of the dual executive, operating within an authoritarian political regime, leads to a slow, drawn-out process of consensus-building, the participants in which are bureaucratic agencies and associated non-state actors. There is a de facto partisan divide of bureaucratic agencies into left and right blocs, which essentially act as representatives of societal constituencies. The president, who in this tradition is credited with setting the general direction of policy, reluctantly has to support one side to end prolonged policy elaboration in which institutional policy-makers fear taking responsibility. The budget process occupies an important place in this policy dynamic, as the annual budget cycle provides impetus for actors to reach decisions (Remington, 2014).

In terms of the aims and capacity of Russian social policy, this article speaks to arguments made by scholars of the Russian welfare state that in conditions of non-democratic politics, social policy priorities are defined by the interests of political and bureaucratic elites, rather than the popular representation of interests (Cook, 2007; Kivinen, in press; Sutela, 2012). Within this line of argument, however, it has been suggested that Russian social spending priorities have oscillated between the fiscal conservatism of the economic and financial bloc, and active social policy associated with the social bloc and 'involving greater amount of funds being made available and targeted for social issues' (Kivinen, in press). This article presents evidence that qualifies this argument. It shows that actors usually viewed as adherents of monetary restraint, such as Aleksei Kudrin, have advocated greater state investment in such areas as education, healthcare and higher living standards. Kudrin sees these as 'productive' areas of social policy, investments in which contribute to the country's 'human capital' and are indispensible for the creation of a knowledge-based economy.[7] This is in contrast to 'non-productive' spending, including unreformed pensions, poorly targeted social benefits and defence.[8]

The article first examines Russian social policy in terms of the interests and ideas of influential policy-makers. It identifies important administrative and policy structures in the social sphere. The process involved in defining indexation rates for *biudzhetnik* salaries, pensions and Maternity Capital, and the freezing of contributions to cumulative pension funds is then considered.

The sources of budget policy-making in the Russian social sphere

The position of key policy-makers on social policy and its funding is a function of their internalised systems of values, expert advice, and interest in popularity and electoral votes. The most powerful actor in the Russian policy process is Vladimir Putin, and his views generally determine the direction of budget policy, including in the social sphere. His fundamental beliefs regarding the economy, specifically fiscal prudence and macro-economic stability, are important for an understanding of the president's policy preferences. Another key component of his outlook relates to the use of Russia's oil and gas wealth to spur economic development and the improvement of citizens' welfare. Those relying on the state budget for their income, such as teachers, doctors, scientists and pensioners, support the president.[9] To these we may add such procedural features of Putin's style of governance as a belief in strategic documents – 'the urge to plan' (Cooper, 2012, p. 1) – and reliance on policy experts working in state ministries and affiliated non-state structures. Connected to this is what we could call 'the urge to integrate', bringing together different levels of authority and policy areas when they bear on a specific problem, a process also mentioned by Cooper (2012, p. 3).[10]

The attention to the social sphere during Putin's tenure has its roots in advice provided to Russia by international institutions in the early 1990s, which was further elaborated in the 'Gref programme' at the start of Putin's presidency (Cook, 2007; Sutela, 2012). The group of experts originally involved in producing the programme were based in the purpose-built Center for Strategic Development (CSR), and included German Gref, El'vira Nabiullina, Yaroslav Kuzminov and Arkadii Dvorkovich. They have remained in prominent state and affiliated positions throughout Putin's leadership. They, together with Aleksei Kudrin, a close colleague of Putin since their days in St Petersburg, have continued to be key defenders of tight monetary policy. This group of top policy-makers remains among the very few 'to whom the president [actually] listens' (Orekhin, 2016a). In 2016 Kudrin re-joined mainstream politics when elected deputy chair of the Presidential Economic Council and put in charge of writing a new strategy for Russia's development post-2018, which might become Putin's next pre-election programme (Khamraev, 2016). As of autumn 2016 Kudrin has taken an active role in the budget process (Kriuchkova & Butrin, 2016a).

Policies developed by this group of reformers, including for the social sphere, were adopted in 2004. Yet, unexpectedly for them some of the measures, particularly the monetisation of in-kind benefits, provoked mass protests by pensioners during winter 2004–2005. Mass demonstrations prompted changes in social policy preferences towards a slower pace of reform and greater state intervention (Remington, 2011; Wengle & Rasell, 2008). In addition, the increase in budget revenues due to rising oil prices allowed extra funds to be dedicated to social issues, producing an 'oil-led' social policy (Cerami, 2009). Yet, decisions on how the extra resources should be spent were determined by policy interests and ideas shared by influential actors at that time. The popular protests threatened the top leadership's hold on power, which made them receptive to the ideas of social scientists outside the narrow circle mentioned above.

The alternative specialists argued that earlier policies failed to address important challenges facing the country: an unprecedented deterioration of living standards, a rapidly worsening demographic outlook, and the unaffordability for the majority of many social goods provided by market structures, including housing (Khmelnitskaya, 2015; Zavisca, 2012). A strong emphasis on social problems and a statist approach to solving them appeared in the presidential address to the national assembly in April 2005 (Putin, 2005), in which the president called for several national priority projects to improve health outcomes and birthrates, as well as educational standards and housing affordability. Cooper (2012, p. 3) traces to this period the interest in developing strategic plans linking Russia's international standing and economic development with demography and social policy.

Introduced in 2006, four national priority projects were supervised by Dmitrii Medvedev and were developed in cooperation with the think tank associated with him, the Institute for Contemporary Development (INSOR) (www.insor-russia.ru/ru/priorities/national_priorities). The projects contributed to Medvedev's popular appeal among voters, including during his presidential term 2008–2012. During his presidency the national projects, formulated as state programmes,[11] became a regular part of the Russian budget (Kivinen, in press).[12]

The electoral cycle of 2007–2008 saw another policy innovation relating to the social sphere, as well as to the wider economy, specifically the creation of what came to be known as 'institutions of development', state-sponsored organisations aimed at leveraging budget funding with private funds for specific policy tasks. In the housing sphere, for instance, two state funds (*fondy*) were set up in 2007 and 2008 (Khmelnitskaya, 2015). In creating these structures policy-makers responded to the view in specialist circles that state intervention is unavoidable as 'poor' apartment owners were unable to afford critically needed major repairs to their apartment buildings. Yet, the populist motives of the ruling elite during the pre-election period should not be overlooked. The poor state of housing and persistent increases in housing charges have consistently been among the most concerning issues for the public (Levada-Tsentr, 2015, p. 9).

Key policy-makers, their interests and ideas in the areas of social spending

The ideological position of Dmitrii Medvedev during his presidency and after has been characterised as a discourse of modernisation, innovation and participatory forms of government. With input from his INSOR advisors and other experts, it is a position which had a significant regime-legitimising effect in the post-GFC environment (Feklyunina & White, 2011). Social policy-making included a rapid increase in benefits and pensions in 2009–2010, evident from Table 1. This could be seen as an anti-crisis measure as recommended by international financial institutions (Kivinen, in press). At the same time, it was reinforced by the paternalistic social ideas of then prime minister, Vladimir Putin. We may also perceive an echo of the advocacy of increased budget spending on 'human capital' in the context of the need to create a knowledge-based economy, something popular among the expert community and to be found in strategic documents written in 2008 and 2012. The increase in spending, described as the '+4 –2 manoeuvre', envisaged greater funding for – in Kudrin's terminology – the 'productive' part of social policy: health and education as well as R&D (Connolly, 2013, pp. 7–8; Cooper, 2012, p. 10), at the expense of unreformed pensions and benefits and military and law enforcement spending. The importance of structural reforms, particularly in the area of pensions, was highlighted. Nonetheless, greater commitments to social spending in the aftermath of the GFC have generated policy challenges in the post-2014 period of budget consolidation.

Despite Medvedev's fascination with innovation-led growth, his personal role in promoting 'active social policy' was modest. He clashed with Aleksei Kudrin, then finance minister in Putin's government, over the growth of military spending. Kudrin resigned in September 2011. Medvedev's influence has been primarily in the sphere of administration and maintaining a balanced policy discourse, with key priorities set within the other part of Russia's dual-executive. For instance, when presenting his report on the government's work to parliament in April 2014 – a month after the takeover of Crimea – Medvedev stressed that Russia has the right to follow its own development path, but noted immediately after that the country nonetheless could not ignore the universal laws of economics (Khamraev & Oktiabrev, 2014).

The emphasis on social policy as a means to invest in the country's human capital that appeared in the late 2000s and has remained strong to the present (Kuzminov, Ovcharova, & Yakobson, 2015), provided the ideational basis for a series of articles published by Putin in 2011–early 2012 and the May decrees of 2012 that set the tone for his third presidential term. Five out of 11 decrees were devoted to social issues: social support, healthcare, education and science, housing, and demographics.[13] Apart from the provision of higher quality services and reaching certain targets for health and educational outcomes, the decrees contained a pledge to raise salaries of *biudzhetniki* – doctors, teachers and scientists – to levels above the regional average and comparable to those in the commercial sector.

Putin's rhetorical commitment to the implementation of the May decrees has been maintained in recent years, but came under pressure during the budget process in 2016.[14] Progress in implementation has been monitored by state-sponsored public organisations such as the All-Russian National Front (*Kommersant*, 2015) and the Presidential Commission on the Implementation of the May Decrees (Kolesnikov, 2016). The sessions (*zasedaniya*) of the Commission have been highly publicised, as were government meetings (*soveshchaniya*) preceding them (Kriuchkova & Manuilova, 2016). This, paired with executive dismissals and resignations – arguably the most visible being the resignation of Vladislav Surkov as deputy prime minister on the first anniversary of the May decrees – and recurring threats to introduce administrative and even criminal responsibility for officials failing to meet decree-related targets (Kozichev & Shelkovnikov, 2016), demonstrates the important legitimacy-seeking element in social policy commitments. It also highlights the difficulty of implementation through reliance on Putin's power *vertikal'* (Monaghan, 2013). During the 2016 budget process maintaining and further increasing *biudzhetnik* salaries became one of the most controversial topics.

In mid-2016, in circumstances of tough negotiations over the new three-year budget, parliamentary elections approaching in September and presidential elections scheduled for 2018, policy-makers' concern for popularity led them to revive the somewhat forgotten instrument of priority projects. Eleven priority projects – not equivalent to the May decrees, but still relating to the social and business environment – were originally to cost the budget R160 billion. This was reduced to R150 billion (1% of budget spending) in the draft budget approved by cabinet on 13 October 2016, while another R100 billion was reserved for various purposes, including the priority projects (http://government.ru/meetings/24877/stenograms/; Butrin, Kriuchkova, & Manuilova, 2016). In nominal terms this is the same as that allocated to the original 2006 national priority projects (Netreba, 2016a); in real terms the present sum of USD2.4 billion is less than half the funding of 10 years earlier (over USD5.5 billion).[15]

In June 2016 a new consultative body, the Council for Strategic Development and Priority Projects, chaired by the president and including important figures from the economic and financial bloc of the government, was set up and began immediate work.[16] Between July and early October six sessions of the Council were held, two of which were chaired by the president. The others, held as meetings of the Council's Presidium, were chaired by Medvedev. At the meetings held in August, it was announced that a new set of priorities would be formulated only in 2017 (Orekhin, 2016a). Yet, by early October 2016, at a session of the Presidium of the Council held at the Sochi Economic Forum, 11 priority projects were discussed. This session of the Council, chaired by Medvedev and with the participation of regional governors, underlined the regional dimension in the 11 priority areas. Medvedev summarised the important electoral rationale behind the projects when he closed the meeting with the following words:

> We need results in the shortest term. You know what I am talking about, and hope you will do all that is necessary. In a year and a half people should be able to feel changes [for the good] in the spheres covered by our projects (http://government.ru/news/24742/).

First Deputy Prime Minister Igor' Shuvalov has been put in charge of the projects' supervision. Shuvalov[17] – a close colleague of Putin since the early 2000s and responsible for the financial and economic bloc of the government – is said to have a major influence over the president. Although seemingly he does not work directly with the social sphere, he supervises the Ministry for Construction (*Minstroi*) and affiliated 'institutions of development' in the housing sphere. Thus, he coordinates the government's work on housing affordability, a key socially-oriented policy issue. His policy position appears close to the fiscal conservatives within the economic and financial bloc. For instance, he has been the driving force behind the recent initiative to 'optimise' the institutions of development. This has meant reduced spending and increased supervision of state corporations and funds. Putin spoke of the need to review these structures in his address to the Federal Assembly in December 2015 (Netreba, 2016b). Work in that direction had already begun earlier in the year with Shuvalov's April directive to reduce spending for the previously mentioned housing funds.[18] Evidence that Shuvalov is pushing optimisation hard is the fact that the construction ministry was the only ministry which undertook the reform and disclosed its spending on development funds, while the Ministry of Economics struggled to get any response from other ministries.

However, Shuvalov's fiscal conservatism co-exists with his close connection to pro-growth actors in and close to the government: presidential advisor Andrei Belousov and members of the Stolypin Club and *Delovaya Rossiya* business association. Belousov was one of the original sponsors of the Agency for Strategic Initiatives (ASI) and has advanced the implementation of its projects. Shuvalov, meanwhile, has worked closely with experts in the housing sphere who participated in such ASI-supervised initiatives as raising Russia's ranking in the World Bank's *Doing Business Guide* (Freinkman & Yakovlev, 2015, pp. 361–362).[19]

Like Belousov, Alexandra Levitskaya is a presidential advisor, but with more direct involvement in social policy. Before her current appointment in 2013, she held senior posts within the government apparatus, at the Ministry of Economics in Putin's government, where she worked with Elvira Nabiullina, Belousov and Andrei Klepach, and at the Ministry of Health in the mid-2000s, when she worked closely with Medvedev on national priority projects (Grishina, Khamraev, & Butrin, 2013). Described in some sources as a close associate of Shuvalov,[20] and as 'one of the most influential female politicians in contemporary Russia, whose experience and opinion are highly valued by the president and the government' (Chemezov, 2014), Levitskaya keeps a low public profile compared to other vocal figures in the social bloc, Ol'ga Golodets in particular. She participates in a great variety of meetings with state and non-state organisations on diverse social issues, including housing, healthcare, childhood protection,[21] youth, the elderly and disabled, as well as civil society development, including philanthropy and volunteering.[22] The last issue received significant attention during the most recent presidential address to the Federal Assembly on 1 December 2016 (Putin,

2016). It is almost never reported what Levitskaya says in these meetings, but she receives high praise from many sources – consider the above quote from Sergei Chemezov. She most likely acts as an important coordinator for social matters in the presidential administration and between it and other parts of the executive. As to whether she supports 'active social policy', and therefore is opposed to budget cuts to 'productive' social sectors, is difficult to say conclusively. It appears likely, though, that like Shuvalov, Levitskaya holds pro-growth policy views.

By contrast, Deputy Prime Minister for Social Issues Ol'ga Golodets, the head of the government's social bloc, is an outspoken public figure. She has a background in labour economics, and worked in executive positions in large private companies (Norilsk Nickel) and regional administrations (Taimyr and Moscow), supervising personnel and social issues. She joined Medvedev's government in May 2012 (http://government.ru/gov/persons/186/bio/). There she supervises matters ranging from family policy and demography, healthcare, education, pensions, to life style and culture. She is a member of the government Budget Commission and presidential commissions and committees, notably the Council for Strategic Development and Priority Projects. In the recent period of budget consolidation Golodets protested against the freezing, cancellation or replacement with one-time payments of respectively *biudzhetnik* salaries, social benefits, Maternity Capital and pensions, as will be discussed below. On such questions she clashed with Anton Siluanov, Minister of Finance, and Aleksei Uliukaev, Minister of Economics, who took rigid positions on the indexation of social spending (Kuvshinova, Liutova, & Papchenkova, 2016). Even when decisions were seemingly taken, as at the 24 June 2016 session of the Budget Commission, Golodets insisted that negotiations continue. Together with other ministers in the social bloc, notably Veronika Skvortsova of the Ministry of Healthcare, Maxim Topilin of the Ministry of Labour and Dmitrii Livanov of the Ministry of Education and Science, Golodets held out against economic and financial bloc pressure and their advocacy of stricter targeting, and the 'scientific' evidence supplied by associated experts on the limited impact of social programmes (Manuilova, 2016a).

In these exchanges, defending 'popular policies' is central, while what is less popular can be sacrificed to spending cuts. The social bloc is prepared to appeal to ideology, arguing that such policies as Maternity Capital (a large cash benefit to mothers with housing policy implications) are the quintessence of the current social priorities of the government, particularly with respect to stimulating births and thus addressing demographic problems. This measure, popular with the public and construed by social bloc officials as existentially important for the country, has been retained – albeit without indexation – in the next three-year budget (Sapozhnikov, 2016).

Protesting too hard, nonetheless, can be harmful, as Minister of Education Livanov learned when he was replaced by Olga Vasil'eva in early September 2016.[23] At a budget meeting (*soveshchanie*) held by Medvedev on 29 July, Livanov presented a report demonstrating that the reduction in spending on education envisaged in the Ministry of Finance's draft documents would cause significant damage to the higher education system and, moreover, would jeopardise the goal in the May decrees of increasing teachers' salaries (Netreba, 2016c). Medvedev suggested that the two ministries resolve their differences between themselves. The process clearly failed, as Livanov resigned on 19 August, and his stance was later dismissed by Medvedev as an attempt to use a difficult situation to score political points.[24] Nonetheless, Livanov's protest against budget cuts resonated with the public and harmed the government's popularity (Netreba, 2016a). As a result, by late summer 2016 Medvedev's position as premier came into doubt. Blunt statements about pensions as quoted at the beginning of this article and comments regarding teachers' salaries in early August did not help.[25] The tension was to a certain degree defused by Livanov's dismissal. Yet, as Levada Centre data show, the government's and Medvedev's personal ratings suffered badly (http://www.levada.ru/2016/12/15/dekabrskie-rejtingi-2/).

While prepared to fight hard over politically sensitive social spending, the social bloc is prepared to be more flexible over those budgetary measures which might be perceived as less 'harmful' in terms of public opinion. In order to increase budget revenues, the social bloc suggested 'learning from Belarus', by introducing a charge for 'non-working' working-age persons to cover the costs of social services used by them. The assumption is that these people are employed in the shadow economy. The suggestion was opposed by the Ministry of Economics as a measure that would immediately run into definitional issues.[26] It and the Ministry of Finance supported a different approach, increasing the efficient collection of social contributions.[27] Other proposals were expected to be more popular with the public, including the social bloc's suggestion to freeze salaries and gradually increase the retirement age for state officials (Manuilova, 2016b). Generally, the Russian public negatively views rises in the remuneration of state officials (Gimpel'son, Mogun, & Brym, 2009, p. 231).

In some of its policy views the social bloc joins with pro-growth actors around the Stolypin Club. Golodets explicitly supports the latter's initiatives, because of the expansion of employment that their 'Strategy of growth' would bring. She also has been involved in consideration of their proposals within the government's inter-departmental working group.[28] Nevertheless, apart from potential gains in employment Golodets has not endorsed the central premises expressed by Stolypin Club members, Sergei Glaz'ev and Andrey Klepach in particular, involving monetary emission and reducing Central Bank base rates to boost business activity (Butrin, 2016a). The social bloc's position is linked with the slow growth model based on internal demand applied in 2010–2013. The financial and economic bloc, as can be seen in the Macro-Economic Forecast presented by the Ministry of Economics to a cabinet meeting on 21 April 2016 and which became the basis for the 2017–2019 budget, aimed specifically to restrain *biudzhetnik* earnings. Their intent was to redirect funds from consumption towards investment (Butrin, 2016b; Manuilova, 2016c).

The position of Aleksei Kudrin – who shares the same ideas as the key figures of the financial bloc, including Nabiullina, Siluanov and Gref in relation to monetary regulation – differs from theirs in relation to personal incomes and social spending. He adds an important 'active social policy' component to the policies supported by the Ministry of Finance and Central Bank. He has insisted on a change of emphasis in social spending priorities, towards those that enhance the development of human capital, and on introducing better means-testing and targeting for other social benefits. This policy, argue Kudrin and a group of experts at the Ministry of Finance's Financial Institute and at the Russian Academy for the National Economy and Public Administration (*RANKhiGS*), would in time generate considerable improvements in living standards (Butrin, 2016a; Manuilova, 2016a; Orekhin, 2016a). As a politician, however, Kudrin has to find ways to increase the popularity of the retrenchment policy. This requires demonstrating 'considerable improvement in living standards' in the very short term. As deputy chair of the Presidential Economic Council from mid-May 2016 and having convened a meeting of 100 important experts in early June (Khamraev, 2016), he (or they) seem to have proposed the re-launch of the priority projects referred to earlier, with the Council for Strategic Development and Priority Projects being formed by the end of June.

Indexation of social payments: salaries of public employees, pensions and Maternity Capital

One of the most contentious questions permeating the budget process has been the indexation of social payments. This section considers how the actors described above interacted in the budget process on this matter. Indexation of social payments is of high electoral salience: the government put off the usual spring amendments to the 2016 budget until autumn, in order to postpone unpopular decisions relating to indexation until after the September parliamentary elections (Visloguzov, 2016b). The indexation of *biudzhetnik* salaries, pensions and such important social payments as Maternity Capital has been the subject of clashes and negotiations between the social and economic–financial blocs of the government. The debate is how much indexation would be affordable in changing economic circumstances, and which categories of social payments should be prioritised.

The pledge to increase *biudzhetnik* salaries – above all teachers, doctors and scientists – was, as noted, part of the May decrees adopted in 2012 and fits with the ideology of investing in human capital. However, as budget revenues dropped by nearly R3 trillion in 2015, a proposal to reduce or forego altogether the inflation-linked 5.5% *biudzhetnik* salary indexation was voiced by Minister of Finance Siluanov in February 2015 (Faliakhov & Kalachikhina, 2015). Yet, in that year the indexation of salaries did go ahead, as the government agreed an anti-crisis plan in which funding for the social sphere increased by 23.5% nominally and 14.4% in real terms (World Bank, 2016, p. 17). The issue re-surfaced during budgetary discussions the next spring, when the government and then the Duma considered the Ministry of Economy's Forecast of Macro-Economic Development. The ministry proposed an investment-led growth model for the 2017–2019 budget, which would restrain income growth in the budget sphere (Butrin, 2016b; Manuilova, 2016c). The aim was to increase the volume of investment in the economy from 3.8% in 2017 to 7.1% in 2019, when it would reach 24.1% of GDP and deliver economic growth of 4.5%. The other side of the 'Russian economic miracle', however, would be the reduction of personal incomes by 3% and pensions by 4.8%. The ministry insisted that the super-tight monetary policy conducted by the Ministry of Finance and CBR aimed at bringing inflation down to 4% in 2017 would soften the adverse effect of income reduction on the public.

The social bloc and Stolypin Club pro-growth actors, as well as those supporting an 'active social policy', strongly disagreed with such an attack on personal incomes. In April 2016 Klepach argued that, while low inflation and economic investment were important, a sharp reduction in social spending would lead to the impoverishment of those in public employment. This would inevitably drive down the quality of their work, which is counterproductive for Russia's growth and competitiveness in the global economy (Manuilova, 2016d). Klepach proposed squaring the circle by increasing public borrowing. Ol'ga Golodets, speaking at the Federation Council in September, was equally disapproving, pointing out that there are working poor in Russia, evident in the salaries of *biudzhetniki*.[29] Kudrin also criticised reductions in spending for education and healthcare, and suggested a threefold increase in borrowing for 2017–2019.[30] Sergei Naryshkin, speaker of the sixth State Duma, in searching for a publically acceptable form of budget cuts, said that the parliament might support freezing salaries of those employed in state administration, but would defend teachers' and doctors' earnings (Manuilova, 2016d).

In the budget draft approved by the government in early October the indexation and raising of *biudzhetnik* salaries contained in the May decrees was left de facto unresolved. Only 30% of funding for this purpose was to come from the federal budget and 70% from regional budgets (Butrin et al., 2016), most of which were already deeply in debt (Zubarevich, 2016). The executive, wary of being decisive on this sensitive issue, shifted the decision-making to the budget's second reading in the Duma in early December. There the Duma's committee for budget and taxation proposed limiting the growth of salaries for doctors to 5.4% instead of the suggested 10.6%. The rationale was to reduce the pressure on regional budgets (which according to the new budget would be credited from the federal budget at below-inflation interest rates) and avoid the situation where, in pursuit of increasing salaries, regions had to lay off teachers and doctors. The first protests against such developments took place in Moscow in late November.[31] The next day a spokesman for Putin reacted by saying that no decision on capping the increase in *biudzhetnik* salaries had been made by the government or president, with the issue still being a matter of '*soglasovanie*' among different policy participants. Golodets then affirmed that doctors' and teachers' salaries would be twice the average regional salary in 2018.[32] The Duma adopted the budget law at the third reading two days following these exchanges, on 9 December. Budget sector employees' salaries will continue to be a battleground in the future.

Another, and for some the most fundamental question of the budgetary process in 2016, was the indexation of pensions. In 2015 pensions were indexed from 1 February at 11.4%. For 2016 Siluanov, as already mentioned, proposed the partial or zero indexation of social payments, including pensions (Faliakhov & Kalachikhina, 2015). Pensions are the biggest cash transfer from the state to citizens in Russia (Remington, 2011). Cash flows within the pension system amount to 9.8% of GDP[33] (see Table 2). Three forms of pension (insurance, social and state) are distributed by the state to 43.2 million people. For the Russian authorities this is a large, politically active social group. The protests following the monetisation of benefits are vividly remembered. The sensitive issue of partial indexation was considered by the government during 2015, and announced by Medvedev at the 7 October meeting of the government's Budget Commission. In February 2016 a partial 4% indexation was paid. It was promised that a second indexation would be paid in the second half of the year, subject to the overall economic and social situation. The social bloc insisted on the second indexation being at the rate of inflation, meaning an indexation of 8.56% from 1 September 2016 (Netreba & Faliakhov, 2016). Yet, over the summer, particularly at the 24 June meeting of the Budget Commission, the Ministry of Finance proposed that the second indexation should

Table 2. Balance of the Pension Fund of Russia, billion rubles.

	2011	2012	2013	2014	2015	*1H16*
Revenues	5255.6	5890.4	6388.4	6159.1	7126.6	*3787.8*
All transfers received	2385.2	2823.3	2851.5	2414.6	3105.2	*1744.8*
Transfers from federal budget	2384.2	2819.5	2846.6	2413.0	3091.7	*1734.9*
Total revenue minus all transfers received	2870.4	3067.1	3536.9	3744.5	4021.4	*2043.0*
Expenditure	4922.1	5451.2	6378.5	6190.1	7670.3	*3768.5*
Deficit (−)/Surplus (+)	333.5	439.1	9.8	−31.1	−543.6	*19.3*

Source: Ministry of Finance, Rosstat and BOFIT.

be replaced by a one-time payment. The social bloc continued to fight against this option during the late summer. The media reported that the final decision was taken personally by Putin and Medvedev.[34] After a government meeting (*soveshchanie*) on 23 August, Medvedev announced that pensioners would receive a one-time payment of R5000 in January 2017, at a cost to the budget of R200 billion.[35] The rationale presented by the Ministry of Finance was that, unlike indexation, the one-time payment would not increase the entitlement base of current pensions, allowing the budget to save R1.3 trillion over 2017–2019 (Netreba & Faliakhov, 2016).

This was immediately followed by the announcement of 'full indexation' in 2017. Defining what 'full indexation' meant took some time. If during the summer of 2016 the Ministry of Finance's plans mentioned 5.9, 4.5 and 4% for 2017, 2018 and 2019 respectively (Netreba & Faliakhov, 2016), in September it proposed a '4–4–4'% formula (Kriuchkova & Butrin, 2016b). The final word was pronounced by President Putin. At a 6 October *soveshchanie* on social and economic issues, Putin demanded full indexation of pensions at the current inflation rate (Kriuchkova & Butrin, 2016b). At the same time, he was receptive to suggestions from economic experts such as Kudrin regarding better targeting and means-testing of social payments. In line with this rationale, in the new budget working pensioners would not have their pensions indexed over the next three years, and pensioners residing abroad would not receive the R5000 payment in January 2017.

In recent years another controversial and related issue has been the freezing of the savings component of the pension system.[36] This measure, first taken in 2013, has changed cash flows in the pension domain and allowed the creation of a 'presidential reserve' fund (approximately R350 billion in 2016). Originally implemented at the insistence of the social bloc, the sum has been used to prop up the Pension Fund (PFR) deficit (see Table 2). According to reports, the money was also used for restructuring the Crimean economy after annexation (Orlov, 2014). In relation to this policy, there were contradictory positions within the economic–financial bloc. While the Ministry of Finance was supportive, Minister of Economics Uliukaev, over the entire period up until his dismissal in November 2016, continued to insist that the money should be used for economic development and previously frozen resources be released (Faliakhov & Kalachikhina, 2015; Orlov, 2014; *Rossia 24*).

Plans for the gradual release of funds were discussed during 2016, accompanied by increased market activity and lobbying by independent pension funds (NPFs). The CBR, interested in forming a long-term funding capacity in the economy, has worked to improve the regulation and operations of Russian NPFs (Aksenov, 2016). The Ministry of Finance, while interested in removing the deficit but realising the importance of the saving component given Russia's aging population, proposed a new scheme called 'Pension capital'. Its key feature was that funds saved by working individuals would remain their property, rather than being the property of the Pension Fund (Fedunenko et al., 2016). Pro-growth actors, Andrei Klepach for instance, while not dismissing this idea altogether, supported Uliukaev's position, insisting that 'defreezing' of the savings component was necessary to restore citizens' trust in the pension system, as well as to provide additional investment for the economy.[37] If a partial release of funds were to go ahead, the NPFs would receive R60 billion in 2017.[38] However, the social bloc was entirely opposed to the proposal, which would redirect revenues away from the Pension Fund. Golodets managed to defend this position during September, following the loss of the battle for a second indexation a month earlier. The Basic Directions of Budget Policy for 2017–2019, considered by the government and the president in early October, included the continuation of the freeze, in which case budget transfers to the Pension Fund in 2017 would grow by R663.1 billion, while total holdings of the Fund would reach R8.18 trillion.[39]

Finally we turn to the indexation of 'Maternity Capital' (MC). Introduced in 2007 it is seen as a way to improve the birthrate by encouraging families to have more than one child. In the mid-2000s the birthrate was 1.3 births per woman. It had reached 1.78 by 2015 (Putin, 2016). The MC has also been a component of Russian housing policy (Khmelnitskaya, 2015), since one of the popular uses of the payment has been to buy property or take out or repay mortgage credit. MC at the time of its introduction was R250,000 and was paid from the Pension Fund. It was subject to annual indexation and by 2015 it had increased to R453,000, costing the Pension Fund R304 billion (Fedunenko et al., 2016). Over the decade of the MC's existence, six million families have benefited and the amount paid was one trillion rubles (Manuilova, 2016e).

The Ministry of Finance's idea to forego the indexation of *biudzhetnik* salaries and social payments affected the MC as well. A debate arose within expert and policy circles regarding its effectiveness with respect to both demography and housing policy. For instance, many reports of fraud involving MC money in the housing market have appeared in the newspapers (Goriacheva, 2016). In the meantime, social policy experts from the Higher School of Economics claimed that such measures were ineffective in stimulating births (Kuzminov et al., 2015; Manuilova, 2016e). RANKhiGS's experts disagreed and advised that the measure should continue as an important instrument of social support for families with children (Manuilova, 2016e; Sapozhnikov, 2016). The economic and financial bloc sided with the HSE experts and tried to eliminate the MC during 2015, a position opposed by the social bloc. Putin, in his state of the nation address in December 2015, supported the social bloc and said that the programme would continue until at least 2019 (Manuilova, 2016e). The debate resurfaced as part of the budgetary process in 2016. In addition to the demands of the Ministry of Economics to close down the programme completely, new suggestions emerged from RANKhiGS specialists that it be means tested and/or divided into regional and federal components. The former component would be paid only in regions with low fertility. This would, for instance, exclude the North Caucasus Federal district where birthrates are high. As the discussion of the 2016 budget and the next three-year budget unfolded the social bloc, particularly the Ministry of Labour, emphasised the excellent results being delivered by the programme (Manuilova, 2016e; Sapozhnikov, 2016). A month later it was confirmed that, as the social bloc insisted, the programme would stay, although without indexation in 2016, leaving the payment at the 2015 level of R453,000. It remains to be seen how long this mass (6 million participants and voters), popular and expensive programme will remain part of the budget. In contrast to the 2015 Presidential address, in December 2016 Putin spoke of 'human capital' when he noted positive trends in Russian demographics; he also referred to 'capital' in a financial sense a number of times. Yet there was no mention of the Maternity Capital programme.

Budget issues in the social sphere are not restricted to indexation. In recent times policy-makers have been busy introducing other measures to both the spending and revenue sides of the social budget. In the housing sphere, important issues include major repairs, territorial development, mortgage funding, and the administration of property and land taxes – the last related to the revenue side of the budget. Structural reforms within the pension sphere – increasing the retirement age, reducing the number of early retirees, increasing the length of the employment requirement, cancelling pensions for working pensioners – as well as improving the collection of social contributions and reducing the shadow part of the economy are topics that have recurred during the budget process over the years, with the recent crisis being no exception. While Putin's moratorium on tax increases during his current term in office has remained in place, certain tentative steps towards institutional reforms have, nevertheless, been taken recently: for example, decisions to increase the retirement age of state administration employees, to exclude the pensions of working pensioners from indexation, and to introduce administrative changes to the collection of pension contributions, to be carried out by the Tax Service from 2017. There is insufficient space in the present article to analyse these developments. Further research is required on how and to what effect Russian bureaucratic and societal actors, while negotiating the current retrenchment of the Russian welfare state (for comparative literature on retrenchment, see Pierson, 1994), went about redefining the institutional foundations of the country's social policy.

Finally, we can briefly compare policy-making over the last two years, with the social and economic–financial blocs pushing against each other while also trying to escape responsibility for tough decisions on social matters, with budget policy-making during the crisis period of 2008–2009. Sutela (2012, p. 164) argues that during that time: '... the debate between fiscal conservatism and development was won by social policy'. Increased social outlays during the period are evident in Table 1. The similarity of the structural background of the two crises highlights the importance of political factors in determining policy-makers' differing responses in the social sphere during 2008–2009 and the recent period. Vladimir Putin's premiership allowed manual control of the Russian government's response to the global financial crisis, the effectiveness of which has been praised by international monetary institutions (Sutela, 2012, p. 227). The authority locus within Putin's government meant that the Russian executive was less divided. Now many influential policy-makers are scattered between its different parts (Nabiullina, Belousov, Klepach, Shuvalov and Levitskaya) and outside it (Kudrin). Moreover, shared ideas regarding social issues as expressed in Concept 2020 and supported by the paternalistic attitude of Prime Minister Putin meant that both the economic–financial and social wings of the government supported the increase in social spending, particularly pensions, introduced in March 2009, including to prop up domestic demand as a response to the crisis (Sutela, 2012, pp. 222–223). This unity was not something the Russian executive displayed during 2014–2016.

Conclusion

The policy process traced in this article approximates the view that policy-making in Russia begins with the president setting the general policy direction, which is followed by bureaucratic stakeholders and affiliated non-state actors becoming locked in battle to determine the details. The social budget policy-making analysed in this article has been primarily concentrated within the executive. There, as far as the social sphere is concerned, the usual distinction drawn between supporters of monetary restraint and adherents of growth policies is not straightforward. While a divide can be drawn between the economic–financial and social blocs of the government, the policy positions of the actors comprising these blocs vis-à-vis the diverse elements of social policy are intertwined in unexpected ways. For instance, Andrei Klepach, associated with pro-growth actors, and Alexei Kudrin, usually considered part of the financial bloc, have both supported increases in public borrowing in order to fund social spending. Together with Golodets, they have resisted freezing salaries for budget sphere employees, a Ministry of Finance proposal. At the same time, the attitudes of these actors towards the targeting of social benefits have varied. If fiscal conservatism, consistently promoted on behalf of the president by the Ministry of Finance, has represented the baseline for the social budget, the positions of other actors have mattered for defining details of current policies and setting future agendas, as with means-testing and targeting. The position of the social ministries led by Vice-Premier Ol'ga Golodets in most cases amounts to resisting budget cuts whenever possible, but being flexible when the political sensitivity of a matter requires it, as in the case of indexation. President Putin interfered in the process only when the most salient and controversial issues were at stake, such as indexation of pensions – but not *biudzhetnik* salaries, which were left as a matter of institutional '*soglasovanie*'. For the president, prime minister and social bloc actors the pursuit of popular policies, that would demonstrate the utmost concern for the public welfare and generate popular support for the political regime, has been paramount.

Notes

1. https://www.youtube.com/watch?v=WSq7oxM_fyo.
2. http://fishki.net/1961862-deneg-net-no-vy-zdes-derzhites-kak-socseti-otreagirovali-na-slova-medvedeva.html.
3. https://www.youtube.com/watch?v=HYB7oDOesg0.
4. The latest official Rosstat figures show that in 2015–2016 the GDP dropped by 3.1%. http://www.gks.ru/wps/wcm/connect/rosstat_main/rosstat/ru/statistics/accounts/#.
5. Rosstat http://www.gks.ru/wps/wcm/connect/rosstat_main/rosstat/ru/statistics/population/level/# and BOFIT.
6. Also see the article by Cooper in this issue.
7. Such views are close to the findings of recent research on the 'developmental state' which has emphasised the importance of a social policy component for successful industrial development (Evans, 2014).
8. Kudrin, speaking at the Sochi Forum, 30 September 2016, https://www.youtube.com/watch?v=HYB7oDOesg0.
9. As well as those working at unprofitable enterprises in Russia's heartland, as long as they have employment and stability (Crowley, 2016).
10. While popular in contemporary public policy thinking and practice, policy integration is a challenging task even in conditions of democracy and a well-functioning civil service. In Russia this approach to policy-making is further complicated by the weakness of formal institutions, lack of accountability and corruption (Huskey, 2009; Monaghan, 2013).
11. For instance the state programme for housing, in its latest version from April 2014, available at http://www.minstroyrf.ru/trades/realizaciya-gosudarstvennyh-programm/29/.
12. Spending on national priority projects and federal targeted programmes can be accessed at http://datamarts.roskazna.ru/razdely/rashody/.
13. The decrees (Numbers 596–606) were signed by Vladimir Putin on 7 May 2012, the day of his inauguration to a third presidential term. As an example, Decree No. 606 on demographic policy is available at http://www.kremlin.ru/acts/news/15257.
14. The real commitment to the implementation of May decrees has not been and could not be complete. Some of the targets set by the decrees – such as a 50% labour productivity increase – had an element of wishful thinking about them and could not be supported by economic reality.
15. Author's own calculations on the basis of figures cited in Netreba (2016a).

16. Members included from the economic–financial bloc: Kudrin, Siluanov, Uliukaev, but also the pro-growth presidential advisor Andrei Belousov and the president of *Delovaya Rossiaya* Aleksei Repik, and the head of the social bloc Ol'ga Golodets. See http://www.kremlin.ru/events/councils/by-council/1029/52297.
17. For biography see http://government.ru/gov/persons/3/bio/
18. See the strategy of development of the joint institution of development in the housing sphere, from 26 February 2016, http://www.minstroyrf.ru/odata/council-of-state/11641/, p. 5.
19. See Igor' Shuvalov and other important actors in the housing sphere – Minister of Construction Mikhail Men', the head of the State Duma housing committee Galina Khovanskaya, and others – at an event at the Institute for Urban Economics, 4 June 2015, http://old.urbaneconomics.ru/news/index213b.html?mat_id=1815#.
20. See http://echo.msk.ru/blog/echo_rating/1504966-echo/.
21. See, for instance, the session of the presidential coordination council for the national strategy for children 2012–2017, http://xn--c1ackabuhcbecyrh.xn--p1ai/news/193.
22. http://www.donorsforum.ru/reports/rabochaya-vstrecha-foruma-donorov-s-sovetnikom-prezidenta-po-voprosam-ekonomicheskogo-razvitiya-i-sotsialnoj-sfery-aleksandroj-levitskoj/.
23. Vasilieva joined the government from the Presidential Administration, where she worked in the department for civic projects.
24. At Government *zasedanie*, 13 October 2016, http://government.ru/meetings/24877/stenograms/.
25. See http://www.rline.tv/news/2016-08-04-vy-zhe-uchitelya-zachem-vam-dengi-sotsseti-kommentiruyut-medvedeva/, 4 August 2016 and https://www.youtube.com/watch?v=QFKiMgrVnYQ.
26. See *Mintrud nameren prorabotat' kriterii dlia platel'shchkov 'naloga na tuneyadstvo'*, 30 September 2016 17:03, available at https://rns.online/economy/Mintrud-nameren-prorabotat-kriterii-dlya-platelschikov-naloga-na-tuneyadstvo-2016-09-30/.
27. They backed the transfer of the administration of pension and other social taxes from the Pension Fund and other extra-budgetary funds to the Federal Tax Service to make the enforcement of tax collection more straightforward, improving the take up and thus budget revenues.
28. See http://stolypinsky.club/2016/08/02/pozitsiya-stolypinskogo-kluba-mne-blizka-golodets-podderzhala-opponentov-minfina/ and http://stolypinsky.club/2016/10/19/titov-programma-stolypinskogo-kluba-strategiya-rosta-v-yanvare-budet-predstavlena-prezidentu/; also see Orekhin (2016b).
29. Sergei Glaz'ev and Andrei Klepach are members of the Stolypin Club presidium (http://stolypinsky.club/prezidium/). In addition, since December 2016 Glaz'ev and Klepach have been on the research council of the newly formed P.A. Stolypin Institute for the Economics of Growth (http://stolypinsky.club/2016/12/21/predstavlena-struktura-strategii-rosta/).
30. *Rossia 24* reporting from Sochi Investment Forum, 30 September 15:54.
31. Pro et contra: Kak uluchshit' kachestvo meditsiny v Rossii?, 6 December 2016, *Kommersant FM*, 20:42.
32. For the Duma's budget committee proposal, Peskov's statement and Golodets' hopes, see http://www.kommersant.ru/doc/3163811, 7 December 2016.
33. According to forecast Pension Fund spending for 2016 (Fedunenko, Zhuravlev, & Shelkovnikov, 2016).
34. See https://www.gazeta.ru/business/news/2016/08/17/n_9007235.shtml.
35. See https://www.gazeta.ru/business/news/2016/08/23/n_9029717.shtml.
36. For the recent – up to early-2015 – history of the issue and the policy process involved see Remington (2015). For the earlier period also see Cook (2007) and Sutela (2012).
37. https://rns.online/economy/Zampred-VEBa-Klepach-ne-verit-v-realizatsiyu-pensionnoi-modeli-Minfina-i-TSB-2016-09-30/.
38. See https://www.gazeta.ru/business/news/2016/09/27/n_9156221.shtml.
39. See https://www.gazeta.ru/business/news/2016/10/07/n_9194969.shtml.

Acknowledgements

The author is grateful to Stephen Fortescue, Markku Kivinen, Vesa Korhonen, Ben Noble and an anonymous reviewer for their assistance and helpful comments on earlier drafts of this article.

Disclosure statement

No potential conflict of interest was reported by the author.

Funding

This research has been conducted as a part of the Centre of Excellence in Russian Studies 'Choices of Russian Modernisation' funded by the Academy of Finland.

References

Aksenov, P. (2016). Oboronka idet k Soglasiu [The military complex is closer to "Soglasie"]. *Kommersant*, 25 April.

Burdyak, A., & Grishina, E. (2016). Income, poverty and prices: Trends of 2016, in Gaidar Institute. *Online Monitoring of Russia's Economic Outlook, 13*, 13–17. Retrieved from http://www.iep.ru/files/text/crisis_monitoring/2016_13-31_july_eng.pdf

Butrin, D. (2016a). Ekonomicheskiy sovet skreplen liuboviu [Economic council is sealed with love]. *Kommersant*, 23 May.

Butrin, D. (2016b). God dobrovol'noy bednosti [A year of voluntary poverty]. *Kommersant*, 10 May.

Butrin, D., Kriuchkova, E., & Manuilova, A. (2016). Obeshchannogo tri goda ne zhdut [Promises remain unfulfilled even after three years of waiting]. *Kommersant*, 13 October.

Cerami, A. (2009). Welfare state developments in the Russian Federation: oil-led social policy and the "Russian miracle". *Social Policy and Administration, 43*, 105–120.

Chemezov, S. (2014). Sovetniku prezidenta Aleksandre Levitskoy – 60 let [Presidential advisor Alexandra Levitskaya has turned 60]. *Nezavisimaya Gazeta*, 14 April. Retrieved from http://www.ng.ru/politics/2014-02-07/2_congrats.html

Connolly, R. (2013). Economic growth and strategies for economic development in Russia. *Russian Analytical Digest, 133*, 5–9.

Cook, L. J. (2007). *Postcommunist welfare states: Reform politics in Russia and Eastern Europe*. Ithaca: Cornell University Press.

Cooper, J. (2012). *Reviewing Russian strategic planning: The emergence of strategy 2020*. Rome: NATO Defense College, Research Review.

Crowley, S. (2016). Monotowns and the political economy of industrial restructuring in Russia. *Post-Soviet Affairs, 32*(5), 397–422. doi:10.1080/1060586X.2015.1054103

Evans, P., 2014, The Korean experience and the twenty-first-century transition to a capability-enhancing developmental state, In I. Yi and T. Mkandawire (Eds.), *Learning from the South Korean Developmental Success* (pp: 31–53). Basingstoke: Palgrave Macmillan.

Faliakhov, R., & Kalachikhina, Y. (2015). Siluanov podrezhet biudzhetnikov [Siluanov will cut down the public sector workers]. *Gazeta.ru*, 11 February. Retrieved from https://www.gazeta.ru/business/2015/02/10/6407849.shtml

Fedunenko, E., Zhuravlev, A., & Shelkovnikov, D. (2016). Chto nuzhno znat' o pensionnoi sisteme Rossii [All you need to know about the Russian Pension System]. *Kommersant-online*, 27 April 17:19.

Feklyunina, V., & White, S. (2011). Discourses of 'Krizis': Economic crisis in Russia and regime legitimacy. *Journal of Communist Studies and Transition Politics, 27*, 385–406.

Fortescue, S. (2016). Russia's "turn to the east": A study in policy making. *Post-Soviet Affairs, 32*, 423–454.

Fortescue, S. (2017). Budget formation in a semi-presidential system. *Post-Communist Economies*, This issue.

Freinkman, L., & Yakovlev, A. (2015). Institutional frameworks to support regulatory reform in middle-income economies: lessons from Russia's recent experience. *Post-Communist Economies, 27*, 354–369.

Gimpel'son, V., Mogun, V., & Brym, R. J. (2009). Weberian ideals vs. Russian reality. In D. K. Rowney & E. Huskey (Eds.), *Russian bureaucracy and the state: Officialdom from Alexander III to Vladimir Putin*, (pp. 231–252). Basingstoke: Palgrave Macmillan.

Goriacheva, V. (2016). Kapital lishili materinskikh prav [The "Capital" has been deprived of its "maternity rights"]. *Kommersant*, 11 May.

Grishina, T., Khamraev, V., & Butrin, D. (2013). Aleksandra Levitskaya okupila terpenie [Alexandra Levitskaya's patience has payed of]. *Kommersant*, 3 August, p. 2

Huskey, E. (2009). The politics-administration nexus in post-communist Russia. In D. K. Rowney & E. Huskey (Eds.), *Russian Bureaucracy and the State: Officialdom from Alexander III to Vladimir Putin* (pp. 253–272). Basingstoke: Palgrave Macmillan.

Khamraev, V. (2016). Aleksei Kudrin gotovit predlozheniya vysokoy stepeni soglasovannosti [Aleksei Kudrin is developing proposals with a high rate of approval]. *Kommersant*, 6 June.

Khamraev, V., & Oktiabrev, A. (2014). Dmitriy Medvedev otvetil na vse svoi voprosy [Dmitrii Medvedev has answered all his questions]. *Kommersant*, 23 April.

Khmelnitskaya, M. (2015). *The policy-making process and social learning in Russia: The case of housing policy*. Basingstoke: Palgrave Macmillan.

Kivinen, M. (In press). Financing the welfare state system in Russia. In C. Aspalter (Ed.), *Welfare regimes in Asia*.

Kolesnikov, A. (2016). Maiskie kushchi [May dreams]. *Kommersant*, 17 May.

Kommersant. (2015). Bollee treti poruchenii iz maiskikh ukazov eshche ne vypolneny [Over one third of May decrees resolutions have not been fulfilled so far]. *Kommersant – online*, 23 December, 16:48.

Kozichev, E., & Shelkovnikov, D. (2016). Chto nuzhno znat' o maiskikh ukazakh [All you need to know about May decrees]. *Kommersant-online*, 16 May, 16:32.

Kriuchkova, E., & Butrin, D. (2016a). Vse vernulos' na drugi svoya [Back to old friends]. *Kommersant*, 22 September.

Kriuchkova, E., & Butrin, D. (2016b). Pushki, pensii, dolgi [Guns, pensions, and debts]. *Kommersant*, 7 October.

Kriuchkova, E., & Manuilova, A. (2016). Otchet po nominalu [Reporting face value]. *Kommersant*, 12 May.

Kuvshinova, O., Liutova, M., & Papchenkova, M. (2016). Biudzhet priniat, no ne poniat [Budget has been adopted but has not been understood]. *Vedomosti*, 26 June.

Kuzminov, Y. I., Ovcharova, L. N., & Yakobson, L. I. (Ed.). (2015). *Social policy: Long-term trends and recent changes*. Moskva: NIU VShE.

Levada-Tsentr. (2015). *Obshchestvennoe Mnenie 2014* [Public opinion 2014]. Moskva: Levada Tsentr.

Maleva, T. M. (Ed.). (2016). *Ezhemesiachnii Monitoring Sotsial'no-ekonomicheskogo Polozheniya i Samochuvstviya Naseleniya: 2015 – iyul' 2016* [Monthly report on socio-economic and welfare development: 2015-July 2016]. Moskva: RANKhiGS. September 2016. Retrieved from http://www.ranepa.ru/images/docs/monitoring/ek-monitoring/monitoring-august-2016.pdf

Manuilova, A. (2016a). Pomoshchi nuzhen kontrol' i uchet [Assistance needs to be counted and monitored]. *Kommersant*, 20 April.

Manuilova, A. (2016b). Chinovnikov ostaviat na rabote. *Kommersant*, 23 April.

Manuilova, A. (2016c). Zarplatnii manevr [Salary trick]. *Kommersant-online*, 10 May, 12:20. Retrieved from http://www.kommersant.ru/doc/2982687.

Manuilova, A. (2016d). Rossii pridetsia narashchivat' dolgi [Russian will have to increase borrowing]. *Kommersant-online*, 19 April, 13:39. Retrieved from http://www.kommersant.ru/doc/2967790.

Manuilova, A. (2016e). U indeksatsii nedetskoe litso [Indexation is not kidding]. *Kommersant*, 19 October.

Monaghan, A. (2013). Putin's Russia: Shaping a 'grand strategy'? *International Affairs, 89*, 1221–1236.

Netreba, P. (2016a). Putin gotovit natzproekty k vyboram [Putin is preparing national projects for elections]. *Gazeta.ru*, 13 September. Retrieved from https://www.gazeta.ru/business/2016/09/13/10191071.shtml

Netreba, P. (2016b). Instituty est', razvitiya net [There are institutions, but no development]. *Gazeta.ru*, 29 August. Retrieved from https://www.gazeta.ru/business/2016/08/29/10164851.shtml

Netreba, P. (2016c). Obrazovanie v Rossii: bez studentov i uchenykh [Education in Russia: without students or scientists]. *Gazeta.ru*, 31 July. Retrieved from https://www.gazeta.ru/business/2016/07/31/9722969.shtml

Netreba, P., & Faliakhov, R. (2016). Kak s"ekonomit' trillion [How to save a trillion]. *Gazeta.ru*, 23 August. Retrieved from https://www.gazeta.ru/business/2016/08/23/10154525.shtml.

Orekhin, P. (2016a). Kogo slushaet president [Who does president listen to]. *Gazeta.ru*, 25 August. Retrieved from https://www.gazeta.ru/business/2016/08/22/10152743.shtml

Orekhin, P. (2016b). Putinomika 4.0 [Putinomics 4.0]. *Gazeta.ru*, 16 August. Retrieved from https://www.gazeta.ru/business/2016/08/12/10122803.shtml

Orlov, A. (2014). Pensii rossiyan ushli v Krym [Russian pensions have gone to the Crimea]. *Gazeta.ru*, 25 June. Retrieved from https://www.gazeta.ru/business/2015/02/10/6407849.shtml

Pierson, P. (1994). *Dismantling the welfare state? Reagan, Thatcher and the politics of retrenchment*. New York, NY: Cambridge University Press.

Putin, V. (2005). *Poslanie Federal'nomu Sobraniyu* [Address to the federal assembly]. 25 April. Retrieved from http://www.kremlin.ru/events/president/transcripts/22931

Putin, V. (2016). *Poslanie Federal'nomu Sobraniyu* [Address to the federal assembly]. 1 December. Retrieved from http://kremlin.ru/events/president/news/53379

Remington, T. (2011). *The politics of inequality in Russia*. New York, NY: Cambridge University Press.

Remington, T. F. (2014). *Presidential decrees in Russia: A comparative perspective*. New York, NY: Cambridge University Press.

Remington, T. (2015). Pension reform in authoritarian regimes: Russia and China compared. Retrieved from https://www.semanticscholar.org/paper/Pension-Reform-in-Authoritarian-Regimes-Russia-and-Remington/af163f68c90759c32c9942e843bc8eb865e7cfc5

Sapozhnikov, O. (2016). Materinskii Kapital nel'zia ni reformirovat', ni uprazdniat' [The 'Maternity Capital' programme can neither be reformed nor dismantled]. *Kommersant-online*, 06 September, 15:52. Retrieved from http://www.kommersant.ru/doc/3082403

Sutela, P. (2012). *The political economy of putin's Russia*. London: Routledge.

Visloguzov, V. (2016a). Defitsit tsveta khaki [Deficit dressed in khaki]. *Kommersant*, 18 October.

Visloguzov, V. (2016b). Gosduma - ne mesto dlia budzheta [The State Duma is not a place for a budget]. *Kommersant*, 13 May, p. 1

Wengle, S., & Rasell, M. (2008). The monetization of L'goty: Changing patterns of welfare politics and provision in Russia. *Europe-Asia Studies, 60*, 739–756.

World Bank. (2016). *Russia Economic Report*. 35, April. Retrieved from http://documents.worldbank.org/curated/en/657991467989516696/pdf/104825-NWP-P156290-PUBLIC-WB-RER-No-35-FINAL-ENG.pdf

Zavisca, J. (2012). *Housing the New Russia*. Ithaca & London: Cornell University Press.

Zubarevich, N. (2016). Regiony Rossii, [Russian Regions] in Institut Gaidara. *Monitoring Ekonomicheskoi Situatsii v Rossii* [Monitoring of Russian Economic Development], *14*, 6–12. Retrieved from http://www.iep.ru/ru/publikatcii/publication/7997.html

The Russian budgetary process and defence: finding the 'golden mean'

Julian Cooper

ABSTRACT

In Russia the budgetary process for defence is broadly similar to that for other sectors but is characterised by a considerable degree of secrecy, limiting the role of parliament and any form of effective social control. The article examines the main actors and features of the defence budgetary process, the system of state secrecy, and explores the issue that generates the most conflict between the ministries of finance and defence, namely the long-term state armament programme.

Introduction

Until the final years of the USSR, military spending was considered a matter of almost total state secrecy and the budget figure revealed each year was deliberately understated to a considerable degree. The real scale of military spending was known to hardly anyone in the country. According to Mikhail Gorbachev, when Yurii Andropov was general secretary of the Communist Party of the Soviet Union, he 'did not allow us (Ryzhkov, Dolgikh and Gorbachev) to approach the budget and data on military expenditures' (Aslund, 1991, p. 191).[1] He later observed: 'All statistics concerning the military–industrial complex were top secret. Inaccessible even to the members of the Politburo … only two or three people had access to data on the military–industrial complex' (Gorbachev, 1997, p. 174). The former leader of the State Planning Committee, Gosplan, Yurii Maslyukov has said that when documents on defence spending were shown to the Politburo members in 1988–1990 the figures were left blank and only written in for them by hand (Nezavisimoe voennoe obozrenie, 2016). With this history it is perhaps not surprising that in post-communist Russia military spending has been regarded as a largely non-transparent matter, with strict limitations on the open publication of data and a budgetary process that provides little if any opportunity for public accountability. The same also applies to the funding of the security services, but this is not surprising as limitations on transparency in this sphere also apply in most Western democratic countries. This article is devoted to the budgetary process in Russia for handling defence spending, the role of the system of state secrecy, and the limits on public engagement in determining the scale of support for the country's armed forces. Overall, the situation today is more open than in Soviet times but much less so than in other developed countries.

Defence spending trends in Russia

Before looking at the budgetary process, to set the scene it is useful to take a brief look at Russian defence spending in recent years and future prospects. Most Russian military expenditure is allocated from Chapter 2 of the federal budget, 'national defence'. However, its scope does not accord fully with the standard definition of defence spending employed by NATO and the Swedish International Peace Research Institute (SIPRI). In addition there is other spending of the Ministry of Defence (MOD) elsewhere in the budget, in particular pensions of servicemen, under the 'social policy' chapter, and spending under such headings as education, health, culture, mass media, found in the relevant chapters, plus budget allocations to other armed forces, in the Russian case the interior troops, formerly under the Ministry of the Interior but now being incorporated into the new Russian National Guard, and the Border Service attached to the Federal Security Service (FSB). But in Russia such spending outside the 'national defence' chapter is not regarded as defence spending so in considering the budget process it is not considered here.

The budget chapter 'national defence' includes personnel costs, operations and maintenance, construction, the development and production of nuclear munitions by 'Rosatom', the procurement of weapons and other military hardware, plus research and development (R&D).[2] Procurement, the repair and maintenance of equipment, and military R&D are funded under the annual state defence order (SDO), the basic scale and content of which is established by the long-term state armament programme (SAP). The current SAP, for the 10-year period 2011–2020, was adopted at the end of 2010 with a total spending of almost 21 trillion roubles, including 19 trillion roubles for the MOD. It is spending of the annual SDO within the framework of the armament programme that has been the principal driver of Russian military spending in recent years, as shown in the Figure 1.

It can be seen that 2015 was a peak year, spending on 'national defence' reaching almost 4.5% of gross domestic product (GDP), compared with 2.8% in 2010.[3] The share of the state defence order reached almost 60%, compared with 37% in 2010. As a share of total federal budget expenditure it increased from 12.6% in 2010 to almost 21% in 2015. At the time of

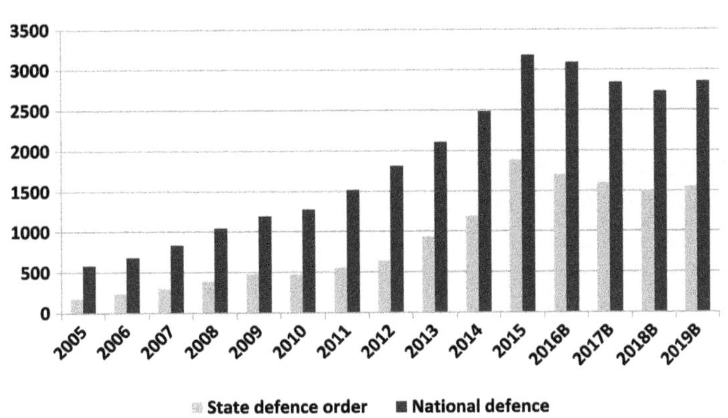

Figure 1. Spending on defence in the Russian federal budget, 2005–2019 (billion roubles). Source: 2005–2015: Cooper (2013, p. 20, 2016b, p. 21); 2016–2019, author's analysis of draft amended budget for 2016 and draft budget for 2017–2019.

Note: 2005–2015 actual spending, 2016–2019 spending in budget, under budget chapter 'national defence'. For comparability, 2016 spending is shown without approximately 800 billion roubles allocated for paying off past debts to the defence industry.

writing, both the draft amended federal budget for 2016 and for the three years 2017–2019 are passing through the budget approval process in the State Duma. They involve a slowdown of the rate of growth of defence spending and spending on the state defence order, as shown in Figure 1, with a reduction of the GDP share to 3.3% in 2017 and 2.9% in 2019, and the state defence order share to 54% in 2019. It should be noted however that the spending intentions for the second and third years of a three-year budget are highly provisional and can be subject to significant later amendment depending on the performance of the economy and policy changes.

Actors in the defence budgetary process

The principal actors engaged in the elaboration of the defence budget are the Ministry of Finance (MOF), Ministry of Defence (MOD), Ministry of Economic Development (MED) and the Military–Industrial Commission (VPK), together with the President, the government and its Commission for Drafting the Budget for the Next Year and the Planned Period, chaired by the prime minister, the State Duma and the Accounts Chamber. The MOF has a department of budgetary policy in the sphere of state military, law and order services, and the state defence order, with staff having the necessary levels of security clearance. It is currently headed by Anatolii Popov, who has had a varied career but no evident earlier experience of military matters (Ministerstvo finansov Rossiiskoi Federatsii, 2016a). Its work is overseen by one of the deputy ministers, Leonid Gorinin, although in the past this responsibility was exercised by the present minister, Anton Siluanov, who fronted for the MOF at the time when the state armament programme to 2020 was being developed and approved in 2010, an experience which must have made him well aware of the issues involved in establishing funding for the armed forces. The MOD has a deputy minister for financial and economic matters, since 2010 Tatiana Shevtsova, before that one of the deputy heads of the Federal Tax Service and as such an appointee of the former defence minister Anatolii Serdyukov. She oversees five departments concerned with the financing of the armed forces and the state defence order, including one for financial planning, directly engaged in the drafting of the federal budget (Ministerstvo oborony Rossiiskoi Federatsii, 2016a, 2016b).

An important role of the MED is supplying the economic forecast on which MOF bases the budget and it also supplies the deflators used to measure price changes in different sectors of the economy for budget planning purposes, including the one used in planning the volume of the state defence order. The ministry does not have a department specifically concerned with defence issues. The VPK is involved in establishing budget funding of the defence industry and its deputy chair and deputy prime minister, Dmitrii Rogozin, tends to be involved in most discussion at a high level of the defence budget. The staff of the VPK form a department of the government apparatus, headed by Igor' Borovkov. This is separate from the government secretariat supporting Rogozin's other activities as deputy prime minister (Pravitel'stvo Rossii, 2016b). At the government level, in the course of drafting a new federal budget, the prime minister usually convenes meetings on specific sectors. Thus for establishing the parameters of the three-year budget for 2017–2019, eight such meetings were held between July and September 2016, including one on funding for the defence industry attended by all the main interested parties, including Rogozin, the deputy defence minister for arms procurement, Yurii Borisov, the ministers of industry, economic development, finance and the general director of Rosatom, responsible for the development and production of nuclear munitions (Pravitel'stvo Rossii, 2016a).

But it is at the presidential level that the key decisions on defence spending are probably taken and not necessarily at formal meetings. Usually at a fairly early stage of the process the President leads discussion of funding in the new budget for the MOD and other power agencies. Thus for the 2017–2019 budget a meeting was held in July 2016 with Sergei Shoigu, Minister of Defence, the Minister of Internal Affairs, the directors of the Federal Security Service and the Federal Service of the Troops of the National Guard, together with Nikolai Patrushev, Secretary of the Security Council, Tat'iana Golikova, chair of the Accounts Chamber, Andrei Belousov, Putin's economic assistant, Konstantin Chuichenko, head of the Control Administration of the Presidential Apparatus, and, of course, Anton Siluanov, Finance Minister. No details of the meeting were revealed, apart from the attendance. However, the brief introduction provides a hint of the nature of the discussion, 'The President held a meeting in the course of which were discussed basic approaches to forming the budget of power agencies in current economic circumstances, with account of the absolute need to ensure national security' (Prezident Rossii, 2016e). Given that the economic situation at the time was not very favourable it can be assumed that Siluanov made it clear that funding would be limited and, indeed, the final draft budget reflected this reality, presumably with the full backing of the President, well known for his consistent support for macroeconomic stability. Much later in the budget process Putin held a meeting with Medvedev and members of the government to discuss budget priorities but little information was provided on the event and who attended, making it impossible to say whether the defence budget may have been one of the topics addressed (Prezident Rossii, 2016c).

Finally, what of non-government involvement in the budget process for defence? First there is the Accounts Chamber, a state agency but with a monitoring role rather than executive. The Chamber provides its assessment of the draft budget at an early stage and this may include comment on the open part of the 'national security' chapter. What is not known, because it will always be classified, is whether it provides a detailed assessment of the defence budget as a whole, including its secret lines of spending. If it does, this must be seen only by the special commission of the Duma established to examine spending on defence and national security, as discussed below.

Study of the defence budgetary process over many years provides little evidence of active involvement by the Security Council. As noted above, its Secretary participated in the meeting with Putin at which the outlines of policy for funding the MOD and other power agencies were discussed in the summer of 2016. However, it is notable that earlier in the year, clearly concerned that the defence budget could be cut, the deputy defence minister for financial matters, Tat'iana Shevtsova, expressed confidence that consideration of defence spending by the Security Council would ensure that the interests of armed forces and the country's security would be protected (Gavrilov, 2016). This could be interpreted as a signal to Anton Siluanov and the MOF that care would be needed in determining the budget for 2017. While the finance minister is a member of the full Security Council, that very rarely meets and he is not one of the limited number of permanent members who meet on a regular basis to consider policy issues. Of this group, there is no representative of the economic bloc of the government, unlike its US equivalent which has the Treasury Secretary as a permanent member. This means that the MOF would only have the prime minister present to represent its interests. This incident suggests that the defence ministry regards the Security Council as the body to which an appeal could be made in the event that a threat appears to the scale of its budget funding. In November 2016 there was some confirmation of this. A few days before the draft budget for 2017–2019 was scheduled to have its first reading in the Duma Putin sought agreement of the Security Council that it should be amended to address an issue of concern raised by the defence committee of parliament in its assessment of the draft, namely the fact that servicemen had not been given the 5000 rouble one-off payment to supplement pensions decreed as available to all the country's pensioners and in the draft budget awarded to the MOD's civilian personnel only (Prezident Rossii, 2016b). According to Putin, Medvedev agreed that the budget had resources to cover the additional cost making it certain that an amendment would be submitted before the second reading. This change may well have been initiated by the new chair of the Duma defence committee, Vladimir Shamanov, a tough, experienced military figure, until shortly before the 2016 Duma elections commander-in-chief of the country's air-borne forces. This change will not appear as an increase in military expenditure, since in Russian practice pensions of servicemen are funded from the 'social policy' chapter of the budget, not 'national defence'.

Independent expertise on the budgetary process for the armed forces of any country tends to be restricted to a fairly narrow circle of specialists working at universities and think tanks, or possibly in the media. Given the extent to which the defence budget is shrouded in secrecy in Russia it is not surprising that the circle is extremely limited. There are hardly any independent experts, the most prominent being Vasilii Zatsepin, head of the laboratory of military economics of the Gaidar Institute for Economic Policy, who writes regularly on military economic issues and often provides informed comment on developments in the wider media. He has a military background and earlier worked at a research institute of the MOD.[4] Another academic expert is Lyudmila Pankova of the Department of Military–Economic Research of Security of the Academy of Sciences Institute of World Economy and International Relations (IMEMO), who occasionally writes on the Russian defence budget (Pankova, 2016).

There are also a few journalists who provide informed commentary on the defence budget, notably Aleksei Nikol'skii of *Vedomosti* and Dmitrii Butrin of *Kommersant*. As part of the budget process academic specialists, usually economists and finance specialists, have an opportunity to make assessments of draft budgets, including comment on the open data relating to the defence budget. Thus there are normally inputs from the Higher School of Economics (HSE), the Presidential Academy of the National Economy and Public Administration (RANKhiGS), the Gaidar Institute for Economic Policy and other institutes. When considering these inputs the Duma Committee on the Budget and Taxes can invite rectors of these institutions to give evidence in person.[5]

What of public opinion? Does the issue of guns or butter concern the wider society? Until a few years ago one would have had to say no, but in the more recent period poll evidence suggests that it now does. Clearly this relates to the public perception that since the annexation of Crimea and the military action in Syria Russia is back on the world stage as a major military power. This enjoys broad public support, which extends to positive attitudes towards budget spending on defence. Thus a VTsIOM (Russian Public Opinion Research Centre) poll in October 2016 asked for views on financing the army. Two choices were presented: 'In the current difficult foreign-political situation ensuring the defence capability of the country has become a higher priority task than other economic expenditures' and 'First it is necessary to ensure the financing of the social sphere, to raise education, health, etc. to an adequate level, then pay attention to defence and security'. The former received the support of 50% of those polled, the latter 35%. At the same time, 58% had a positive assessment of the defence industry, believing that it contributed to the development of the economy, while 27% believed it did not (VTsIOM, 2016a). It is interesting that over time the proportion of people believing that more money should be spent on the armed forces has declined, but this may well be because of a mounting perception that the forces have become better equipped and less in need of more money. Thus in 2008 75% of those polled supported the position that the forces needed more funding, declining to 68% in 2010 and 55% in 2014 (VTsIOM, 2014). At the same time, public support for the armed forces has increased, from only 32% in December 2006, to 56% by the end of 2008 (i.e. after the Georgia war), 65% in December 2013 and 82% in October 2015 (i.e. the beginning of Russian military action in Syria) (VTsIOM, 2016b). The extent to which public opinion has any impact on policy for the defence budget is impossible to judge.

Stages of the defence budgetary process

For those not familiar with the budgetary process it may be helpful at this stage to consider briefly the actual procedure according to which MOF, with MOD, drafts the defence budget. On the basis of MED's economic forecast and the established spending priorities of the President and government MOF sets general spending limits which are communicated, together with other information such as relevant deflators to plan spending over the three-year period, to all budget holders, including the MOD, which then elaborate their own draft budgets. Thus for the draft budget for 2017–2019 the MOF's methodological instructions issued in July 2016 included a specific direction for the MOD that spending in nominal terms had to be reduced by 6% in each of the three years, whereas most other ministries and department had to find larger savings of 9% and 11% in the second and third years (Ministerstvo finansov Rossiiskoi Federatsii, 2016b). The process of compiling the budget is simplified by the wide use of 'norms', standard rates for the use of consumables such as food, uniforms, fuel and lubricants. The MOD, like all 'power' agencies, has an officially approved number of personnel, its *shtat*, which is used to calculate the need for many kinds of consumables. However, this methodology is favourable to the MOD or other agency if its actual number of personnel is below the level of the *shtat*, creating slack in the budget and easing financial constraints. It is known that in recent years the actual number of servicemen in the MOD has been less that the specified one million, perhaps to the extent of 200,000. This may well be an important factor in the MOD's ability to operate within the apparently tight budget limits set by the MOF and may help to explain why the relationship between the two ministries in the routine budget process appears to be relatively free of significant conflict. Once MOF has prepared the draft budget, incorporating the MOD's draft, which has probably been amended after discussion between representatives of the two ministries, it is approved by the government and submitted to the State Duma for approval. Once it has passed though all three readings it goes to the Federation Council which ratifies the Duma's decision, making possible the budget's signing into law by the President.

Is the budget for defence amended as it passes through the Duma approval process and, if so, by how much and who is responsible? This can be established by comparing the original draft federal budget with the final version adopted as law. Amendments to the volume of funding are possible during the second reading. Taking the budget chapter for 'national

Table 1. Change in total volume of spending on 'national defence' from the first draft budget to the budget signed into law (%).

2005	2006	2007	2008	2009	2010	2011	2012	2013	2014	2015
+0.4	+1.3	0.0	+6.0	−5.1	0.0	+0.1	−0.4	−1.5	−0.8	+4.7

Sources: Relevant webpage of federal budget for each year on State Duma website: http://asozd2.duma.gov.ru/ and annual report of Federal Treasury on budget implementation which gives allocation in final budget law, http://www.roskazna.ru/ispolnenie-byudzhetov/

defence' over the years 2005–2015, the extent to which the total allocation has been changed is shown in Table 1.

It can be seen that in most years there are changes but of a relatively minor character. However in three of the 11 years the changes were larger, to the extent of approximately 5%. This tended to happen in years of economic uncertainty and almost all the changes were initiated by the government itself, not individual deputies. If these changes affected the classified part of the spending, they will have been seen only by members of the special Commission charged with handling classified data.

Secrecy and the defence budget

Before looking in detail at the defence budget and its passage through the State Duma it is necessary to consider the issue of secrecy. As this issue has been discussed by the present author elsewhere, here only the principal features will be considered (Cooper, 2013, pp. 33–36). According to the law on the state secret, the fundamental document governing matters of secrecy, there are three levels of 'secret' (*sekretno*), 'top secret' (*sovershenno sekretno*) and 'of exceptional importance' (*osoboi vazhnosti*). In the federal budget two categories of secrecy apply. Taking the example of the 2013–2015 budget, only 26 of its detailed appendices were open, 10 were 'secret' and eight 'top secret'. In the case of the draft budget for 2017–2019 the number of classified appendices had increased to 22. The secret appendices provide details of spending on defence and national security considered unsuitable for open publication, including the detailed budgets of the security services, probably 'top secret', and the annual state defence order, although between 1992 and 1997 and again in 2004 and 2005 some aggregate details were published openly. It is likely that such details are now 'secret' but there may well be a 'top secret' appendix with a detailed breakdown of spending by specific weapon programmes.

What constitutes a state secret is set out in a list of data considered secret, originally dating from 1993 but updated many times since. In relation to the defence budget, there is no direct indication that data on planned expenditure on the armed forces are secret. Indeed, the law of 1993 specified that the only budget expenditures to be considered secret were those devoted to intelligence, counter-intelligence and counter-terrorism activities. There is explicit reference to secrecy in relation to indicators of the state defence order for armaments and other military hardware, but from the context – a section on the economy, science and technology – it was until recently not clear whether the monetary value of the order was such an indicator (Cooper, 2013, p. 34). In the latest amendment of the list in February 2016 this ambiguity, which the author drew attention to in 2013, was eliminated. The list of data considered secret was amended to tighten restrictions on revealing details of new weapons under development and in particular data revealing in monetary terms expenditures on orders for the development, production and repair of armaments and other military hardware (Konsul'tant Plyus, 2016). This means that even the limited data made available earlier on the state defence order as part of the budgetary process are now considered a state secret, making it extremely unlikely in the foreseeable future that it will once again be published openly. If this new restriction applied only to development programmes for genuinely new, original weapon systems that Russia wished to keep secret for a period, then the measure would not be out of line with international practice. But to apply it to all systems renders any social control over a large part of the defence budget impossible. In their assessment of the draft 2017–2019 budget, experts of the Russian Academy of the National Economy and State Service (RANKhiGS), together with those of the Gaidar Institute of Economic Policy, called for the removal of the 'secret' classification of the appendices on the state defence order, restoring their publication as in the years 2002–2005, and called on the inter-agency commission on the protection of the state secret, charged with determining policy on secrecy, to review the principles of protecting financial and economic data with a view to ensuring a greater degree of transparency (Gosudarstvennaya Duma, 2016a).

There is another dimension to secrecy in relation to the budgetary process for defence and security. Those handling secret data receive financial 'compensation', meaning that there are many with a material interest in at least maintaining the existing level of secrecy and perhaps also extending the range of data subject to classification. This is a legacy of the USSR that has been given new life in post-communist Russia. State officials in the Soviet Union received increments to their pay for handling secret data, their scale depending on the level of secrecy of the data concerned. It has been claimed that this measure was at least in part intended to reduce the turnover of staff having regular access to state secrets but was probably also to compensate for limitations on such personnel such as restrictions on foreign travel. The system was reinstated in Russia by a decree of 1994 which introduced a 25% supplement to pay for those with permanent access to data 'of exceptional importance', 20% if 'top secret' and 10% if 'secret'. This would have applied to those staff of the ministries of finance and defence handling budget data considered secret and to other government officials also having access. In 2006 this decree was replaced by a new one 'on granting social guarantees to citizens permitted access to state secrets on a permanent basis'. The supplements to pay were sharply increased: now 50–75%, 30–50% and 10–15%, respectively. The variation depended on the volume of data handled and the time period over which it was considered secret (Cooper, 2013, p. 35). It is worth noting that this new, more generous, regime was adopted at a time when Aleksei Kudrin, now an opponent of secrecy in relation to defence spending, was Minister of Finance.[6] However, the change was probably introduced at the insistence of the security services and supported by President Putin and the then prime minister Mikhail Fradkov, who went on to become director of the Foreign Intelligence Service (SVR), with little scope for opposition in government circles. This system is not one conducive to greater transparency in budgetary matters, especially in relation to defence and security.

It is considerations of secrecy that shape the budgetary process for defence in the State Duma. Not all deputies have access to the full version of the federal budget. The classified appendices setting out the full spending of the MOD and details of the annual state defence order are only available to those with the appropriate security clearance and such deputies tend to have military and security backgrounds. This severely limits the possibility of deputies without such backgrounds exercising control on behalf of the wider society. During the 1990s and early 2000s there were a few deputies, members of opposition parties of democratic orientation, in particular 'Yabloko' and the 'Union of Right Forces', able to participate in the budget process and advocate a greater degree of transparency. In this respect Aleksei Arbatov stands out, a deputy of 'Yabloko' between 1993 and 2003 and a highly respected academic specialist on military matters. In recent years, especially since 2007, when 'Yaboloko' has had no deputies in the Duma, public pressure for greater openness has weakened.

To review classified spending in the draft budget the Duma appoints a special commission with deputies who must have security clearance to examine materials covered by the law on state secrecy. Thus at an early stage in the work of the newly elected Duma in October 2016 a Commission for examining expenditures of the federal budget directed to providing for national defence, national security and the state defence order was established consisting of 21 deputies, seven each from the committees for the budget and taxes, defence, and security and countering corruption, with the three committee chairs as co-chairs of the Commission. According to the decree establishing the Commission, it is 'For securing the necessary degree of confidentiality and personal responsibility for retention of state secrets in looking at draft federal laws on the federal budget'. Study of the background of the deputies reveals that while the deputies from the budget and taxes committee mainly have backgrounds in finance, those from the defence committee have backgrounds in the armed forces and those from the security committee in the judiciary or security services, one being a former director of the FSB, Nikolai Kovalev (SZRF, 2016). Only this small group of deputies has the right to see the classified budget spending for defence and national security. In the words of a former Duma deputy, Dmitrii Gudkov, all the rest have no choice but to take it as a given fact and 'push buttons', i.e. to vote for the allocations regardless (Khachaturov, 2016).

Over the past decade the share of classified spending in the Russian federal budget has steadily increased, mainly because the secret component of the defence budget has grown, as shown in Table 2.

It will be seen that the share of secret spending increased rapidly from 2013. This can be explained largely by the rapid growth of spending on the annual state defence order as the ambitious state armament programme to 2020 was implemented, both being classified. However, there was also some increased spending under another classified programme, a federal targeted programme for the development of the defence industry.

Russia is not alone in having classified spending but its share of the defence budget is exceptional. The USA is well known for its classified 'black' defence budget spending but its share of the total budget is much smaller than in Russia. Thus in 2015, according to an informed account, it was almost 12% of the total defence budget (The Daily Beast, 2014). However, its size, $59 billion, was larger than Russia's total 'national defence' spending in that

Table 2. Extent of classification of spending in the budget chapter 'national defence' in the budget law, 2005–2015 (%).

2005	2006	2007	2008	2009	2010	2011	2012	2013	2014	2015
42.1	42.8	45.3	46.1	48.1	46.4	46.9	47.6	52.6	58.8	67.6

Sources: 2005–2014: Zatsepin (2015, p. 558). 2015 federal budget before amendment: calculated by author from documentation on budget law, http://asozd2.duma.gov.ru/main.nsf/(Spravka)?OpenAgent&RN=611445-6

year if valued at the November 2016 exchange rate ($48 billion), which provides a telling insight into the comparative scale of Russia's defence effort.

On transparency of defence budgets generally, according to Transparency International, Russia is far from being the country with the least transparent regime. In its 2011 report, *The Transparency of National Defence Budgets*, which examined in detail the practices of 93 countries, Russia was found to be in the group of 20 with moderate to high transparency, well ahead of such countries as China, Saudi Arabia, Nigeria and Pakistan rated as having low transparency (Transparency International UK, 2011, p. 6). The rating is based on an examination of the treatment of defence in the budgetary process of each country according to 20 different criteria. However, these do not include an assessment of the share of the budget that is classified and in the author's view the assessment is probably too favourable to Russia. One interesting issue is that Russia is not alone in having a parliamentary process that involves the examination of the defence budget in details only by a specially formed committee with the authority to do so: this is also the case in France, Greece and Poland (Transparency International UK, 2011, p. 13).

There are institutions other than the State Duma that have the right to examine classified spending in the budget as it goes through the approval process and after the budget is implemented. The principal one is the Accounts Chamber (*Schetnaya palata*), headed since 2013 by Tatiana Golikova. All work concerning classified spending for defence and national security is overseen by the deputy chair of the Chamber, currently Vera Chistova, who has long experience of the finances of the defence industry and the armed forces, being in 2009–2010 deputy minister of defence for financial and economic issues (Schetnaya palata Rossiiskoi Federatsii, 2016). Under her supervision is the department for expert-analytical and control activities in the field of expenditure on national defence, security, and law and order, headed by Vasilii Boitsov, who has an industrial background (Moskovskii fiziko-tekhnicheskii institut, 2016). Needless to say, the reports on its activities are classified.

According to Evghenii Gontmakher, a leading member of the of Committee of Civic Initiatives, there are other bodies that have the right to examine matters concerned with defence and other classified spending, notably the Control Directorate of the Presidential administration and the equivalent special department of the government apparatus, but the results of their verification work are not made public. Summarising a review of the handling of classified budget data in Russia, he concludes, 'This system of closure (*zakrytosti*) includes an enormous number of diverse institutions. It is self-sufficient, everything is there, right up to culture. It is a large slice of our state life, I consider surplus' (Khachaturov, 2016).[7]

Where serious differences arise: the state armament programme

The principal clashes between the MOD and MOF on spending arise not so much with the annual budget but with the largest item of spending, the volume of funding of the state armament programme (SAP). This is not the budgetary process as such, but in the case of defence a crucial dimension of the relationship between the armed forces and the economic bloc of the government. The SAP is a 10-year document setting out intentions over the period for the development and procurement of new armaments and other military hardware, plus repairs and modernisation of the existing stock of weapons, with more detail for the first five years than for the second. Normally, the programme is updated and extended every five years (Cooper, 2012, pp. 170–174). There were serious differences of opinion when deciding the funding of the first Russian armament programmes in 1996, 2002 and 2006, but more serious was the clash between the MOD and MOF in the run up to approval of the SAP covering the period 2011–2020. The MOD sought total funding of 36 billion roubles; the MOF aimed at 13 billion roubles. In the end, President Medvedev and Prime Minister Putin backed a total of more than 20 billion roubles, notwithstanding the evident dissatisfaction of Finance Minister Aleksei Kudrin. After the brief war with Georgia there was clearly an understanding at the top level of the political and military leadership that modernisation of the equipment of the armed forces could no longer be delayed even though the process would place a heavy burden on the budget. Later in 2011, after openly voicing his opposition to the scale of defence spending with the approval of the new SAP, Kudrin was dismissed by Medvedev. The SAP was elaborated on the basis of an optimistic economic forecast. In the event, the performance of the Russian economy turned out to be much less favourable than was expected but commitment to the SAP remained firm, with a mounting share of budget spending devoted to defence.

At the time of writing there is once again a standoff between the MOD and MOF on funding the SAP, now its successor, a programme for the years 2018–2025. With a faltering economy, strains on the budget, the impact of NATO and EU sanctions following the Russian annexation of Crimea and military action in Ukraine, plus the ending of Ukrainian supplies to the Russian defence industry, and delays in a number of programmes for the development of major new weapons, it was decided to postpone the start of a new SAP from 2016 to 2018.

Before this postponement, which was decided in January 2015, Sergei Shoigu, Minister of Defence, revealed that a total of 55 trillion roubles had been considered but after completing work on rationalising the range of armaments and military hardware to be procured it had proved possible to reduce the sum to 30 trillion roubles (Ministerstvo oborony Rossiiskoi Federatsii, 2014). With the decision to postpone and a still unfavourable economic situation in September 2016 a meeting was convened by Putin to resolve the question of funding. A week later more details of this closed meeting emerged, as described by Ivan Safronov, *Kommersant's* well-informed correspondent. MOF Siluanov and MOD Shoigu were unable to agree an acceptable volume of funding for GPV-2025 and the issue was unresolved at the end of the meeting with serious disagreement remaining. According to a source in the financial bloc of the government, after an opening report by Rogozin discussion between the parties developed 'in raised tones'. Siluanov stood out for total funding of 12 trillion roubles; Shoigu for 22 trillion, which clearly represented a retreat from the 30 trillion that the MOD had been seeking earlier, even with the reduction from 10 years to eight. Not surprisingly, Siluanov stressed the state of the economy and the fact that increased defence spending would have a negative impact on the realisation of other priorities, including social. The military focused on the need to ensure the country's national security (Safronov, 2016). In September 2016, speaking at a meeting at the 'Kalashnikov' concern in Izhevsk, Putin made clear his general thinking on defence spending:

> Naturally, there are always issues between the capabilities of the state, budget options and the needs of the Armed Forces. Here we must find the golden mean so that our defence spending does not crowd out other needs linked with social issues, social welfare, pensions, healthcare and education – many areas for which the state and the federal budget are responsible. This is why we must find this golden mean (Prezident Rossii, 2016d).[8]

Given the scale of the gap between the MOD and MOF on the next SAP, it may require Putin to take a final decision, which will reveal his understanding of where the golden mean is to be found.

But all participants in the debate are aware that Putin has been warning the defence industry for some time that it must prepare for smaller state defence orders as the basic task of modernising the weaponry of the armed forces is completed, allowing transition to a more modest annual rate of renewal in order to maintain the 70% share of modern hardware that has been the principal target of SAP to 2020. Speaking at the Congress of the Union of Machine Builders in April 2016 he said that the peak load of the state defence order will come 'next year' and urged defence companies to diversify their activities and manufacture more high technology civil goods (Prezident Rossii, 2016f). He has reiterated this theme on several occasions since and has been echoed by Rogozin and Deputy Defence Minister Borisov.

Openly expressed serious discontent with policy on funding the armed forces has been rare in recent years. During the 1990s, when budget funding of the forces was extremely limited, it was common, but with improved budget support, especially since the start of the SAP to 2020, the implementation of which has resulted in quite significant increases in military spending on a year-to-year basis, there has been little criticism of the MOF from the military and its supporters in the media. It is also noticeable that within the government the MOF alone has at times questioned the resource commitment to defence. But discussion of the new SAP has to some extent changed the situation, giving the guns versus butter issue a wider public airing. The most striking example occurred in August 2016 with outspoken criticism of the finance ministry in the pages of *Voenno-promyshlennyi kur'er*, a weekly widely read in military, defence industry and security circles and having a strong patriotic, at times nationalistic, orientation. One of the paper's leading journalists, Oleg Falichev, launched an attack on the 'anaconda' of the Ministry of Finance, intent on squeezing to a minimum funding on the new SAP. He noted MOF's wish to devote 12 trillion roubles to the programme, not the '24 trillion' requested by MOD (although as noted above the sum actually requested was 22 trillion). In his view the bureaucrats of MOF were guilty of voluntarism, taking no account of the real national security imperatives facing Russia. 'Russia de facto lives in the conditions of an armed camp', he asserted. President Putin was clearly expected to resolve the matter in favour of the military (Falichev, 2016). In the same issue there was a more authoritative article on the same theme by no less than Vasili Burenok, the director of the MOD's 46th Central Research Institute, responsible for drawing up the SAP and establishing the methodology of its compilation. Under the heading, 'State programme of disarmament', he openly acknowledged that work on the programme was being delayed by a clash of opinion between the economic and 'power' blocs of the government. He attempted to demonstrate that analysis of the equipment needs of the armed forces, above all the MOD, was a scientific process which revealed what was essential to ensure the country's national security. The funding requested by the MOD for the GPV was not an arbitrary (*sluchaino*) figure but firmly substantiated, and to question it was to put the country's security at risk. Perhaps aware that his argument had been unconvincingly technocratic, Burenok then went on to underline the importance of the work of the defence industry for the development of the economy. He concluded,

> ... the SAP is not only a document aimed at ensuring the defence capability of Russia, but also in its own way a locomotive of the development of industry and the scientific potential of the country. Reduction of the volume of financing relative to the substantiated level will bring about the most negative consequences both for national security and for the industrial development of the country. This cannot be permitted (Burenok, 2016).

These interventions of Falichev and Burenok probably give a flavour of arguments that were then being conducted in the corridors of power. They were not alone in warning of the dangers of reduced defence spending at a time of perceived external pressures on Russia. One of the most tireless advocates of maintaining a strong military, opposed to any reduction of spending, is the leader of the Communist Party of the Russian Federation, Gennadii Zyuganov. In October 2016 he made it clear that his party, together with 'Just Russia', would oppose any cuts in spending and threats to the funding of the 2018–2025 SAP (RIA Novosti, 2016).

Conclusion

The defence budgetary process in Russia has many features in common with that for other types of government expenditure. However a significant portion of military spending is subject to classification under the country's strict secrecy regime and this limits the role of parliament and the wider public. All State Duma deputies can have a say on open defence spending, but only a very limited number with appropriate security clearance have access to the large 'black' spending, in recent years constituting more than half of the total defence budget. Secrecy also imposes very strict limits on the ability of experts, journalists and the public to monitor military spending and exert any form of democratic social control. The Accounts Chamber does have access but almost all its reports relating to the defence budget are classified. In recent years the 'guns versus butter' issue has become more acute in Russia because of the determination of the country's political and military leadership to make good many years of meagre funding that made it impossible to supply the armed forces with new weapons. As modernisation progresses a moderation of the growth of defence spending is now in prospect. President Putin now has the task of persuading the military that a golden mean must be found.

Notes

1. Nikolai Ryzhkov, Vladimir Dolgikh and Gorbachev were at the time Politburo members.
2. On defence spending in the Russian federal budget see Cooper (2013).
3. On military spending trends, their sources and implications, see Cooper (2016a).
4. See his contribution to the Gaidar Institute's annual reviews of the development of the Russian economy, e.g. Zatsepin (2015).
5. As did the rectors of HSE, Yaroslav Kuz'minov, and RANKhiGS, Vladimir Mau, in November 2016 for discussion of the draft 2017–2019 budget (Gosudarstvennaya Duma, 2016b).
6. Kudrin expressed his astonishment and disapproval of the fact that so much spending in Russia's 2016 budget was classified (Lenta, 2016).
7. The reference to culture is probably because the funding of cultural facilities under the security services is classified, as Gontmakher earlier in the article notes.
8. Putin reiterated this view at a meeting of the MOD leadership later in the year: '… our military development and equipment modernisation work must proceed in strict accordance with the principle of what is reasonably sufficient and in accordance with our country's economic possibilities. We must carry out this work while at the same time continuing to move towards our set economic growth targets, developing civilian production sectors, and guaranteeing fulfilment of our social sector obligations. There must be no contradictions here. All of these different areas must be in natural coordination and must complement each other' (Prezident Rossii, 2016a).

Disclosure statement

No potential conflict of interest was reported by the author.

References

Aslund, A. (1991). *Gorbachev's struggle for economic reform* (2nd ed.). London: Pinter Publishers.

Burenok, V. (2016, August 31). Gosprogramma razoruzheniya. Finansovoe vedomstvo ekonomit na natsional'noi bezopasnosti [The state programme of disarmament. The financial agency economises on national security]. *Voenno-promyshlennyi kur'er*, no. 33. Retrieved from http://vpk-news.ru/articles/32056

Cooper, J. (2016a, June). The military dimension of a more Militant Russia. *Russian Journal of Economics, 2*, 129–145.

Cooper, J. (2016b, March). *Russia' state armament programme to 2020: A quantitative assessment of implementation 2011–2015*, FOI Report, FOI-R-4239-SE, Swedish Defence Research Agency.

Cooper, J. (2013, September). *Russian military expenditure: Data, analysis and issues* (FOI Report, FOI-R-3688-SE). Swedish Defence Research Agency.

Cooper, J. (2012). Military procurement in Russia. In R. N. McDermott, B. Nygren, & C. Vendil Palin (Eds.), *The Russian armed forces in transition. Economics, geopolitical and institutional uncertainties* (pp. 169–189). London: Routledge.

Falichev, O. (2016, August 31). Anakonda Minfina [The Minfin anaconda]. *Voenno-promyshlennyi kur'ier*. no.33. Retrieved from http://vpk-news.ru/articles/32069

Gavrilov, Yu. (2016, April 4). Rubl' ushel v oboronu [The rouble has gone into defence]. *Rossiiskaya gazeta* (interview with Tat'iana Shevtsova).

Gorbachev, M. (1997). *Memoirs*. London: Bantam Books.

Gosudarstvennaya Duma. (2016a). RANKhiGS i Institut ekonomicheskoi politiki im. E.T. Gaidara, Zaklyuchenie na proekt Federal'nogo zakon "O federal'nom byudzhete na 2017 god in planovyi period 2018 i 2019 godv" [Conclusion on the draft federal law "on the federal budget for 2017 and the plan years 2018 and 2019"] (pp. 22–23). Retrieved November 9, 2016, from http://asozd2.duma.gov.ru/main.nsf/(Spravka)?OpenAgent&RN=15455-7

Gosudarstvennaya Duma. (2016b). Retrieved November 10, 2016. http://www.duma.gov.ru/news/273/1777541/#photo1

Khachaturov, A. (2016, October 19). Byudzhet-2016 - eto bomba! [Budget 2016 is a bomb!]. *Novaya gazeta*. The reference to culture is probably because the funding of cultural facilities under the security services is classified, as Gontmakher earlier in the article notes.

Konsul'tant Plyus. (2016, February 28). Ukaz Prezidenta RF ot 28.02.2016 N 90 "O vnesenii izmenenii v perechen' svedenii, otnesennykh k gosudarstvennoi taine, utverzhdennyi Ukazom [Edict of President of RF of 28 February 2016 no. 90 "On making changes in the list of data referred to state secret, approved by edict].

Lenta. (2016, October 4). Kudrin udivilsya rasshireniyu sekretnykh statei byudzheta Rossii [Kudrin is astonished by the expansion of secret articles of the budget]. Retrieved from https://lenta.ru/news/2016/10/04/kudrinsurprise/

Ministerstvo finansov Rossiiskoi Federatsii. (2016a). Retrieved November 06, 2016, from http://minfin.ru/ru/ministry/structure/director_department/?id_4=103

Ministerstvo finansov Rossiiskoi Federatsii. (2016b). Pis'mo Minfina Rossii ot 21.07.2016 No.16-01-08/42065, "Predstavlenie glavnymi rasporyaditelyami sredstv federal'nogo byudzheta predlozhenii po raspredelenie byudzhetnykh assignovanii na 2017 god i na planvyi period 2018 i 2019 godov" [Letter of Minfin Russia of 21 July 2016 n.16-01-08/42065, "Presentation by main managers of means of the federal budget of proposals for the distribution of budget allocations for 2017 and plan years 2018 and 2019"], *Metodicheskie ukazaniya* [Methodological guidelines], p. 3. Retrieved November 10, 2016, from http://minfin.ru/ru/perfomance/budget/federal_budget/budgeti/11-16/index.php#

Ministerstvo oborony Rossiiskoi Federatsii. (2014, December 19). Otchet na rasshirennom zasedanii kollegii Minoborony Rossii ob itogakh deyatel'nosti za 2014 g [Report of extended session of the board of the Ministry of Defence on results of activity in 2014]. Retrieved from http://function.mil.ru/news_page/country/more.htm?id=12004148@egNews

Ministerstvo oborony Rossiiskoi Federatsii. (2016a). Retrieved November 06, 2016, from http://structure.mil.ru/management/deputy.htm

Ministerstvo oborony Rossiiskoi Federatsii. (2016b). Retrieved November 6, 2016, from http://structure.mil.ru/structure/ministry_of_defence/details.htm?id=9905@egOrganization

Moskovskii fiziko-tekhnicheskii institut. (2016). Vasilii Borisovich Boitsov. Retrieved November 14, 2016, from http://mba.mipt.ru/page-faculty.html

Nezavisimoe voennoe obozrenie. (2016, October 28). Kakim putem poidet rossiiskaya oboronka. Glavnye stat'i voennykh raskhodov ostayutsya pod sekretom [By which path will Russian defence go. The main articles of military spending remain secret]. *Nezavisimoe voennoe obozrenie*. Retrieved from http://nvo.ng.ru/realty/2016-10-28/2_924_red.html

Pankova. (2016). 2016 Russian Defence budget: Key problems and possible solutions. In A. Arbatov & S. Oznobishchev (Eds.), *Russia: Arms control, disarmament and international security*. IMEMO supplement to the Russian edition of the SIPRI Yearbook 2015 (pp. 127–145). Moscow: IMEMO. Retrieved from http://www.imemo.ru/files/File/en/publ/2016/Supplement_2016.pdf

Pravitel'stvo Rossii. (2016a, July 28). O raskhodakh federal'nogo byudzheta na 2017–2019 gody v chasti razvitiya oboronnoi promyshlennost [On outlays of the federal budget for 2017–2019 with respect to the development of the defence industry]. Retrieved from http://government.ru/news/24039/

Pravitel'stvo Rossii. (2016b, November 28). Podrazdelenii Apparata Pravitel'stva [Subdivisions of the apparatus of the government]. Retrieved from http://government.ru/office/structure/

Prezident. (2016a, November 16). Soveshchanie s rukovodstvom Ministerstva oborony. Retrieved from http://en.kremlin.ru/events/president/news/53262

Prezident Rossii. (2016b, November 8). Soveshchanie s postoyannymi chlenami Soveta Bezopasnosti. Retrieved from http://www.kremlin.ru/events/president/news/53217

Prezident Rossii. (2016c, September 28). Soveshchanie po voprosam formirovaniya byudzheta [Meeting on questions of forming the budget]. Retrieved from http://kremlin.ru/events/president/news/52978

Prezident Rossii. (2016d, September 20). Vstrecha s rabochimi kontserna "Kalashnikov" [Meeting with workers of the 'Kalashnikov' concern]. Retrieved from http://www.kremlin.ru/events/president/news/52921

Prezident Rossii. (2016e, July 12). Soveshchanie po voprosam formirovaniya byudzheta silovykh struktur [Meeting on questions of forming the budget of power structures]. Retrieved from http://www.kremlin.ru/events/president/news/52498

Prezident Rossii. (2016f, April 19). 'S"ezd Soyuza mashinostroitelei Rossii' [Congress of the union of machine builders of Russia]. Retrieved from http://www.kremlin.ru/events/president/news/51746

RIA Novosti. (2016, October 22). Zyuganov: sokrashchenie raskhodov na oboronu mozhet skazat'sya na perevooruzheniya [Zyuganov: reduction of outlays on defence may tell on rearmament]. Retrieved from http://ria.ru/defense_safety/20161022/1479787269.html

Safronov, I. (2016, September 17). Esli ne skhod, to razval [If don't get off, then a breakdown]. Retrieved September 17, 2016, from http://www.kommersant.ru/doc/3092628

Schetnaya palata Rossiiskoi Federatsii. (2016). Retrieved November 04, 2016, from http://www.ach.gov.ru/structure/chistova-vera-ergeshevna/

SZRF. (2016, October 24). *Sobranie zakonodatel'stva Rossiiskoi Federatsii*, no. 43, Postanovlenie Gosudarstvennoi Dumy Federal'nogo Sobraniya ot 19.10.2016 g. No.42-7 GD [Decree of State Duma of Federal Assembly of 19 October 2016, No.42-7 GD].

The Daily Beast. (2014, March 6). Read the Pentagon's $59 Billion 'Black' budget'. Retrieved from http://www.thedailybeast.com/articles/2014/03/06/inside-the-pentagon-s-59-billion-black-budget.html

Transparency International UK. (2011, October). *The transparency of national defence budgets*. London: Author.

VTsIOM. (2014, April 29). Vooruzhennye sily Rossii: obshchestvennaya otsenka [The armed forces of Russia: public evaluation]. Retrieved from http://www.old.wciom.ru/fileadmin/news/2014/army_wciom_2014.pdf

VTsIOM. (2016a, October 12). 'Armiya: moral' i tsennost' [The army: morale and values]. Retrieved from http://infographics.wciom.ru/theme-archive/politics/internal-policy/political-ideology/article/armija-i-obshchestvo.html

VTsIOM. (2016b, February18). Armiya Rossiya-2016 [The army, Russia 2016]. Retrieved from http://wciom.ru/index.php?id=236&uid=115586

Zatsepin, V. (2015). Voennaya ekonomika i voennaya reforma v Rossii [Military economy and military reform in Russia]. In *Rossiiskaya ekonomika v 2014 god. Tendentsii i perspektivy*. Moscow: Institut ekonomicheskoi politiki imeni E. T. Gaidara.

Russian experts: missing actors of the budget process

Lev Jakobson

ABSTRACT
This article provides an examination of the role of experts in the Russian budget process. Experts are those whose role is based on specialised knowledge and technical skills, rather than affiliation to an agency, association or political party. Ideally their contributions are impartial. In the first part of the article the channels of expert influence are described, primarily within the executive branch. Features are found in these channels that mean that impartial advice is not always guaranteed. In the second part, on the basis of a survey of experts, the answers to two questions are sought: whether they feel that impartial advice is expected of them and whether they provide it. There are negative elements in the responses on both counts, suggesting that despite some evidence of demand for such advice on the part of policy-makers, expert advice is often not impartial.

Introduction

The budget process provides a forum for regular competition between a complete set of politically represented vested interests. While a collision of interests within the budget process might be less dramatic than a change of government or legislative conflict, the latter events do not happen often and involve a relatively limited number of actors. Using the terminology of Rhodes (1997), specific issue networks move into the limelight in such situations, whereas analysis and interpretation of the budget process provide a wider view of the policy community, as well as of how it functions.

Researchers of Russian political life traditionally focus on relationships between the key figures in various government agencies and with the business community (Rutland, in press; Sakwa, 2011; Yakovlev, 2014). However, as studies of other countries have demonstrated, experts have also had a major impact on policy-making in various areas in recent years. They have acted both as official and unofficial advisers to decision-makers and parties in all sorts of public and private discussions. Often expert bodies (committees, boards, etc.), which do not have decision-making authority, have nevertheless played a key role in seeking a balance of interests (Puetter, 2007). Competition between advisers and officials, of whom the latter should be much more influential according to their formal status, has been the subject of major controversy in the UK and Australia (Rhodes, 2008, p. 334). It is unlikely that such phenomena and their underlying problems are less important in Russia where, as some researchers believe (Ledeneva, 2013), informal governance factors and issues play a major role.

Experts are those members of the policy community whose membership is based primarily on the acceptance of their knowledge and analytical skills by other participants. Their role is unique in that they are expected, in theory at least, to display the maximum possible degree of independence from ideological positions and private interests in their contributions to political deliberations. This stands in sharp contrast to the expectations of all other participants, who are called upon to act as exponents of value-laden ideas or vested interests and who are likely to be concentrated in political parties, trade unions, business associations, etc. Experts position themselves as the most coherent proponents and mouthpieces of a technocratic approach to politics.

An analysis of the assumptions, conditions and implications of expert involvement in policy-making provides an insight into that side of the process which is not reduced to actions more or less prescribed by the legally guaranteed status of elected politicians, civil servants and official lobbyists. No one occupying any of those positions can be described as an expert in the sense the word is used here, no matter how brilliant an economist, political scientist or whatever they might be. For any other well-qualified specialist the role of expert is in principle available. It need not be the individual's only role, and certainly does not have to be a lifelong vocation. In many countries it is not unusual, for example, that retired senior officials act as influential experts. The same role is played by journalists and academics, if they are speaking on issues that are not directly connected with the interests of their employer. It is common for business people to be members of expert committees. Needless to say, they, like any other expert, must reveal any conflict of interest. But for an expert, as for an official, the possibility of a conflict of interest requires the individual to step back from their role only in specific circumstances, not that they refuse the role altogether.

The fundamental definitional requirement of an expert is, then, impartiality. However, we know from evidence from Western countries that the capacity and willingness of members of the political community who present themselves as experts to act in practice as absolutely neutral 'honest brokers' are far from guaranteed (for example, Pielke, 2007). Whether there is a gap between the assumed and actual behaviour of experts is a question clearly of no less significance for countries in which the functioning of the policy community is less structured and formalised than in the West. This applies to post-communist countries, in particular Russia.

Moreover, a peculiarity of Russian political discourse in the economic sphere is a tendency to avoid explicit confrontation between the ideological positions and interests of various social groups. The chapters devoted to the economy of nearly all political party programmes and the attitude of the country's leadership to economic issues largely focus on economic growth, technological progress, the protection of the national economy from undesirable external influences and structural shifts seen as beneficial to the population at large. Such discourse implies a significant demand for politically neutral, impartial and competent judgements which are free from any lobbying. To the best of the author's knowledge there is no previously published research devoted to the issue of the extent to which and how such demand is met.

This article intends to at least partially fill this gap. It attempts to provide answers to the following questions: does Russian reality provide any indication of an emerging demand for experts who possess the above qualities? What is the institutional framework of this demand and how effectively does it address the demand? What is the supply of expert judgements and does it satisfy the demand?

A negative answer to the first question implies that economic policy discourse is more likely to be non-transparent than transparent, and therefore not very susceptible to outside analysis. If the answer to the question is positive, however, the answers to the subsequent questions could be quite helpful in determining how adequate the decision-making process is. Indeed, it would make sense to find a way to head off the risk of what could be referred to as comfortable delusion. This is a situation in which decision-makers, while reserving the right to disagree, want to receive carefully prepared and reasonably independent opinion and might believe that they are receiving it. But experts prefer to avoid judgements that they believe might be unwelcome to clients. In these circumstances, an expert discourse on economic growth, efficiency or the like could well distort rather than inform the content of policy, including in the eyes of those who make it.

The involvement of experts in Russian political life has been discussed in a number of publications (Balayan & Sungurov, 2016; Belyaeva, 2013; Belyaeva, Yena, Zaytsev, & Chulok, 2016; Yakovlev, Freinkman, & Zolotov, 2016). However, they are mainly focused not on the characteristics of the experts and the expert community per se but rather on the environment in which they operate. The authors of most studies more or less openly advocate what they see as the corporate interests of the expert community and think tanks by focusing on an assessment of the correspondence between those interests and the reality of the environment in which they work. The analyses provide grounds for a legitimate criticism of experts' work environment, but they devote much less attention to a critical assessment of the qualities of the experts themselves. One such critical assessment is the study by Jakobson (2008), which evaluated the role of experts as 'voices' of civil society. It showed that as many complaints could be addressed to the way experts play their role as to the conditions in which they are required to operate.

Overall, the literature does not provide any substantial analysis of the role of experts in generating Russian economic policies. We do not claim an exhaustive coverage of the issue here, and the three questions above are discussed with two major limitations.

First, the questions are assumed to refer solely to the budget process rather than to the entire range of economic policies. The budget process, owing to its specific nature mentioned in the beginning of the article, is more appropriate for an analysis of the role of experts than any other decision-making process related to the national economy. Here the budget process is examined in both a narrow and a broad sense. The former is a set of procedures explicitly set out in the Budget Code. The latter covers any other actions by members of the policy community capable of significantly, and sometimes critically, affecting decision-making in respect of the budget.

The second qualification is that the opportunities for evidence-based analysis of experts' participation in various discussion platforms are unequal. For example, experts' participation in informal meetings with the President may be perceived as more significant than their membership of ministerial public councils. The available data, however, push us in the direction of the more formalised and more easily recorded forms of expert participation, that is, the latter over the former. Given that, it is important to account for differences in the degree of transparency of the various channels of expert influence on the budget process, broadly defined, now to be described.

Channels of influence

Since the budget provides the forum for the balancing of a large range of aggressively promoted interests, its content is unlikely to be satisfactorily explained if our field of view is intentionally narrowed, for example, to what takes place in the parliament in its autumn budget session. To provide exhaustive answers to the questions that this article purports to answer, one would have to follow the activity of experts through all the various parts of the budget process in the wider sense. The problem is that not all activity is observable to the same degree, and one's focus is inevitably on the most visible components of the process. Nevertheless, to the extent possible it is necessary to draw attention not only to official and transparent channels of expert influence but to those less obvious.

The various forms, forums and channels of expert influence on the budget process are now outlined, before in the second part of the article, an analysis of the expectations and self-assessment of expert activities, based on a survey of experts, is presented.

Individual experts and expert institutions

While in this article I am dealing with experts as individuals, it should be noted that more often than not they work for institutions with expert status. A comprehensive study of expert influences on the budget process would include this institutional element. While that is not attempted here, a few comments are offered. Firstly, policy advice and even whole policy programmes are sometimes presented to the government, whether publicly or in private, in the name of an institution. Secondly, institutional affiliation often but not necessarily says something about the general policy orientation of individual experts. Thirdly, the influence of individual experts often depends on the influence of the institutions which employ them. That in turn is a function of many factors, from the circumstances in which an institution is operating, through who set it up and the nature of its funding, to the personal contacts of its leading figures. When Russia was seriously in debt to international and foreign creditors, representatives of the IMF and other foreign institutions had a significant influence on Russian budget policy. Today one will not find evidence of such influence. Such a change undoubtedly affected the influence of experts working for those institutions, many of whom moved to jobs in Russian educational institutions, government research centres, and policy-oriented think tanks. And while initially independent think tanks in the area of economic policy-making relied on foreign funding or big business, subsequently they came to rely ever more on government support. That included a number of well-established, previously independent organisations becoming structural units of such major institutions as the Russian Academy of the National Economy and Administration or the Higher School of Economics. Other expert institutions deeply involved in the budget process are the Financial Research Institute of the Ministry of Finance and the independent Economic Expert Group.

Personal relationships

A form of relatively non-transparent and informal expert influence derives from contacts between officials and experts with common professional and personal backgrounds. From this perspective, it is particularly notable that in post-Soviet Russia more ministers have come from the expert community than from among members of parliament, although, having said that, fewer former experts now hold top jobs in the government system than 20 or even 10 years ago. However, there is no doubt that such former experts as Deputy Prime Minister Arkadiy Dvorkovich, presidential economic advisor Andrei Belousov and Central Bank Chair Elvira Nabiullina maintain close links with the expert community. And dozens of people have followed the expert–major decision-maker–expert path. Notable examples include acting Prime Minister in the first years of Yeltsin's presidency, the late Yegor Gaidar, and the recent Finance Minister Aleksei Kudrin. The latter continues to play an important role in economic policy-making, despite his dramatic move from the status of senior official to that of expert. The opinions of such experts undoubtedly remain authoritative for people still in power with whom they worked, particularly those who they themselves recruited. A turn as an expert need not occur only at the beginning and end of one's career, but can also come in the middle. Former Minister of Economic Development Aleksei Uliukaev's path was expert–high-ranking official–expert–high-ranking official–minister.

Each person's biography says something about their personal relationships. In the case of close professional contacts in the area the person was responsible for in government, they will probably have a sizable effect on decision-making.

Public forums

Three channels of influence that are rather more open to public view than the purely informal contacts described in the previous paragraph can be identified, even if despite their public nature their actual impact is not easy to trace. First are articles, including op-eds, by experts or interviews with them in the mass media. Second are the numerous, crowded economic forums which have become fashionable in Russia recently. They are initiated and organised by federal and regional authorities as well as large business associations and corporations. Though designed to promote business development and attended largely by business people, such forums devote a substantial part of their agenda to discussions between government officials and experts. This can be seen in the agendas of recent forums well attended by government members (https://www.forumspb.com/ru/2016/sections/62/materials/309; http://www.forumkuban.org/ru/glavnaya-stranitsa/). Third are official parliamentary hearings. According to the Russian Federation State Duma website, expert opinions were presented at all hearings relating to the budget and tax issues starting from 2012 (www.komitet-bn.km.duma.gov.ru/site.xp/050048.html).

Involvement at executive level

The bulk of the budget formation process takes place within the executive, and it is there that we find expert involvement of a kind which warrants more detailed attention.

Experts are involved in drawing up the strategic policy documents that inform detailed budget formation. Since 2000, working groups set up on the instructions of the President or Prime Minister to deliberate on strategic issues in the area of economic policy have been regular practice. While often these groups include experts along with government officials, two of the most widely publicised economic reform programmes – the so-called Gref programme http://www.budgetrf.ru/Publications/Programs/Government/Gref2000/Gref2000000.htm) and 'Strategy 2020' (http://2020strategy.ru/documents/32710234.html) – were developed by groups composed almost exclusively of experts operating on the basis of instructions issued by Vladimir Putin. Both of these documents concentrated on budget policies. However, the recommendations put forward by the experts in these cases were implemented only partially and inconsistently. Thus, the proposal to dramatically raise the wages of teachers, doctors and some other public sector workers in 'Strategy 2020' was included in Putin's 2012 presidential campaign promises and then the so-called May Decrees, in which form they continue to play a major role in budget formation. At the same time the proposal in the same document to increase the share of allocations to education, health and some other items at the expense of defence spending was not supported. This lack of consistency combined with lower budget revenues caused by the recession resulted in major budget policy tension.

Another such programme – specifically focused on encouraging a higher growth rate – is currently under preparation, in a process being led by Aleksei Kudrin and a number of expert economists who could be described as being in the 'liberal' camp, but with economists from the more stimulus-oriented Stolypin Club also involved.

Once the process moves beyond broad strategy, experts are involved in the preparation of specific budgets. This is the case at the very preliminary stages, including drafting budget proposals for ministries, regional administrations and other government agencies. Each of these agencies has its own pool of experts involved in the calculation and substantiation of funding requests.

Arguably the most used channel for the involvement of experts in the budget process is the activities of various institutions created by the authorities as a kind of bridge between government and society. While some institutions of this sort have existed for some time, their number – as well as the variety of their functions and agendas – has grown exponentially over the last 10 years. As far as can be judged, this development is in pursuit of two goals. One can be called technocratic and the other political. The first is to improve the quality of decisions, using qualified independent expert evaluation. The second is to strengthen the power of feedback from the community. While international researchers have focused mainly on the federal and regional public chambers (*obshchestvennye palaty*) (Evans, 2008; Richter, 2009a, 2009b; Stuvøy, 2014), other institutions – particularly presidential and governmental councils and some other public agencies – equally warrant attention. Some of them have a mixed composition, including experts, government officials and members of parliament. This is primarily true of councils under the President of Russia and regional governors.

Presidential councils exert probably the heaviest clout of all the institutions in question, with their membership approved directly by the President who also chairs their meetings. Experts are present in most such councils, albeit normally in small numbers (http://kremlin.ru/structure/councils). Their presence cannot be explained by PR considerations, not least because the debates carried on at their meetings do not receive media coverage. Council meetings result in presidential instructions (*porucheniia*), to be implemented by executive authorities as a matter of priority and invariably supported by the dominant parliamentary faction. In many cases, compliance with instructions will require funding and, therefore, preparation and adoption of the underlying decisions turn out to be a major and integral part of the budget process defined in a wider sense. However, because of the already mentioned confidential nature of the debates, it is difficult to assess experts' specific contribution to decision-making through presidential councils.

The aforementioned Public Chamber (*Obshchestvennaia palata*) at federal level was set up in 2005 under a special law. Leaving aside those aspects of its operation discussed in the articles cited above, it is worth making two points. First, a good number of its members are experts in our sense, while it also has a wide pool of officially appointed experts who are not part of its structure and who perform the role of external experts. Second, under a 2009 law, all socially important draft laws are to be reviewed by the Public Chamber. While the law does not define the criteria for a draft to qualify as socially important, the draft budget and other laws relevant to the budget process are undoubtedly included. Though the review serves only for guidance, the authorities are required to acknowledge its findings.

Thus, what we see is a legally protected channel for the compulsory involvement in the budget process of the experts associated with the Public Chamber. The most notable use of this channel was the so-called 'zero readings' of the draft budget held by the Chamber from 2011 to 2014. The information published on the Chamber's website (https://www.oprf.ru/) suggests a fairly critical approach to budget policies and contains proposals for major amendments, including the reallocation of funds between the federal and regional budgets. Having said that, there is no evidence in the approved budgets that these proposals were taken into account.

In 2015, the Chamber did not hold zero readings on the 2016 budget, though it used its right to do so in respect of 40 other laws. While some of them relate to budget policies, they generally do so only marginally, the approval of tax benefits for donations to endowments and cultural activities being an example (https://www.oprf.ru/1449/2133/1537/2142/newsitem/30553). That seems to be an issue of special interest to the Chamber's members, who are predominantly NGO leaders with a wide representation of cultural figures. It could be said that in 2015, there was a shift away from the more general and sometimes critical evaluations of the budget observed in the past towards real but nevertheless narrow, minor and self-interested influence.

The trend continued in 2016, although, unlike the previous year, the budget was approved by the Chamber as a whole rather than line by line. However, only two of the recommendations posted on the Public Chamber website (https://www.oprf.ru/press/news/2016/newsitem/37130) directly concerned budgetary allocations. One recommended an increase in government support for NGOs, while the other concerned changes in the distribution of profits from the sale of liquor to the regional budgets. Two other recommendations vaguely suggested improvements in the methodology of expenditure planning and the measurement of cost effectiveness.

The government's Expert Council, established in 2012, provides a way for the expert community to participate in preparing and implementing decisions of the government and federal executive authorities, including through both proposing issues for discussion by the prime minister and other government members and the review of issues once on the government agenda (http://open.gov.ru/event/5598185/). Coordinating the Council's proceedings is one of the main functions of the Minister for Open Government Affairs. The Expert Council currently has 364 members, with several hundred experts taking part in the proceedings of its 34 working groups (http://government.ru/department/270/members/). Judging by its website, the Council regularly provides opinions on issues directly or indirectly related to budget policies and has been charged since 2015 with reviewing the efficiency of budget performance under a special instruction of the prime minister (http://open.gov.ru/expert_sovet/). The published opinions contain numerous recommendations on amending the draft decisions under review. However, a random analysis suggests that only some recommendations are implemented.

Budget policy reviews are carried out by public councils established in 54 of 73 federal executive agencies. Under a Government Resolution, these councils are required, in particular, to review draft government programmes the funding for which accounts for more than half of budget expenditures (http://www.consultant.ru/document/cons_doc_LAW_134737/). In 2014 and 2015, to judge by the councils' minutes published on their websites, they reviewed 21 draft programmes. In 18 cases, the drafts were approved without recommending any significant changes to funding. In the other three cases, the public councils pointed to the inadequacy of funding if the programme's proposed objectives were to be met. In all these cases – the Health, Housing and Social Welfare programmes – these objectives related to the needs of the population at large. The public councils of the respective ministries responsible for these programmes recommended considerable increases in funding, something clearly in the interests of the ministries. However, the recommendations were not implemented.

While one might expect the most important contribution to the evaluation of budget policies to come from the Public Council of the Ministry of Finance, judging by its 2015 and 2016 agendas it did not review draft budgets either in general or by major revenue and spending lines. The council was more concerned with various draft ministerial resolutions and guidelines, as well as staff work plans and performance reports (http://minfin.ru/ru/om/os/). In sum, regarding activities which had the potential to affect budget revenue and expenditure allocations, the public councils were either fairly passive or unsuccessful in lobbying for more funding for their parent agencies.

The experience of the above institutions shows that the existence of official, legally guaranteed channels for expert involvement in the budget process does not guarantee intensive use of these channels. But the fact that they have been created, at considerable cost including the time spent by officials in dialogue with experts as part of the said institutions, suggests that the authorities feel a real need for independent evaluation which is not adequately satisfied. It is true that the demand comes from the top governance level, which is where the decisions are made to create these institutions, while at lower levels cooperation with experts might be regarded as an unpleasant extra duty. As another explanation, the institutions could serve as window dressing for electors. However, if this were the case, they would have been more visible in the media, election rhetoric, etc. There is little such visibility, just as there is no indication that the public at large holds the expert community in high esteem.

We might gain some further clarity as to the current state of affairs, by looking within the community itself and at its perceptions of the demand of government and society for impartial and competent analysis.

Expert advice: biased demand, biased supply

In February and March 2016, a survey of 304 experts from 24 Russian cities was conducted under the author's guidance, in the form of face-to-face interviews based on a questionnaire developed jointly by the author, Irina Mersianova and Aleksandr Kinsburgsky. Glas Naroda, an independent pollster, was contracted by the Higher School of Economics to conduct the interviews. The developers of the survey contacted members of the government's Expert Council, as well as a number of other experts known by their publications in the media. The interviewers then contacted those who consented to participate in the study. In selecting

Table 1. Extent of the authorities' interest in various aspects of expert activities, according to expert respondents (%).

	Strong interest	Medium interest	Weak interest	No interest
Provision of objective information	16	57	20	5
Advice on how to explain the authorities' actions	38	33	18	7
Advice on ways to implement specific priorities identified by the authorities	32	38	20	7
Offering proposals on strategic change	12	37	36	13

Table 2. The expert qualities most important in working with decision-makers and in promoting one's authority in the eyes of the mass media and general public, according to expert respondents (%).

	Working with decision-makers	Promoting authority in mass media and general public
Ability to understand the specific interests of the client and readiness to take them into account	53	17
Knowledge of the facts, being well-informed	41	51
High intellectual level, analytical skills	33	37
Ability to present one's position clearly and with flair	31	57
Efficient work methods	31	27
High work rate	22	8
Thorough and diligent analysis and presentation	21	12
Knowledge of the literature in one's professional field	12	9
Pursuit of objective truth, independence and impartiality in one's evaluations	11	20
Integrity	7	14
Willingness to be guided by ideals in forming views on specific issues	3	6

Table 3. Respondents' judgements on the frequency of representation of various interests (%).

Interests	Very often	Quite often	Quite rarely	Never	No answer or undecided
Big business	17	51	24	1	8
Small and medium business	4	29	55	4	8
Education, healthcare, science, culture, etc.	4	35	49	7	5
Workers	2	9	47	32	10
Civil servants	4	21	43	20	11
Military personnel	6	38	38	7	11
Pensioners	8	31	45	9	8

the respondents, we took special care to include some who cooperated with opposition parties rather than the government, although the latter prevailed in the sample. While we cannot claim that the sample is representative, since the extent and composition of the overall population of experts is unknown, the presence of opposition-linked experts among the greater number with government links is a reasonable reflection of the composition of the expert community itself. All our respondents had considerable experience in expert review activities and good knowledge of the actors involved and underlying conditions. This allowed us to regard them as in some sense 'experts on experts'. On that basis and without overestimating the accuracy of the specific quantitative parameters of our findings, we believe them to be fairly informative.

An obvious disadvantage of relying on the survey data is that it is impossible to gauge if the respondents' opinion corresponds to reality. Given the fact that the questions referred to activities in which the respondents were engaged, one cannot be sure that their opinions were not emotion-laden. As we will see, the respondent experts have been quite critical of their colleagues' professional qualities and activities. The advantages of relying on the survey data include the chance to access perceptions of what is going on in the not so transparent channels of expert–government interaction. We did not think it wise, though, to ask direct questions about informal or less obvious channels because the answers may have been unreliable. However, the data presented below provide an insight into how experts fulfil their role, even if it is not possible to gauge the relative importance and effectiveness of formal and informal channels.

The respondents were asked to assess both the demand for and supply of unbiased competent advice. Table 1 shows responses to a question regarding the interest of the authorities in various aspects of expert activities.

As can be seen from the table, the great majority of the surveyed experts perceived that the authorities were interested in receiving what could be described as assistance in pursuing particular actions. However, interest in receiving strategic advice that might question the advisability of those actions is perceived as being much weaker. The respondents were also asked whether they believed that the authorities' interest in expert advice had changed since the mid-2000s. In this regard, 42% of those interviewed answered that interest was greater, 29% asserted the opposite, 22% saw no change and 7% gave no answer. Interestingly, Moscow-based experts and those from other regions expressed fairly diverging views on this question, with stronger interest reported by less than 40% of the former and 59% of the latter. This can hardly be explained by the fact that regions pay more heed to experts than Moscow. Rather, it is because such dialogue is a relative novelty for regional authorities while in the capital it is well-established though not always effective.

Moscow-based and regional experts also differed in their opinion on whether the authorities took the advice of the most competent and impartial experts into account. While 54% of all respondents were positive in this respect, only half of Moscow experts were as compared to 69% outside Moscow. This can be explained, apart from the relative novelty of such activities in the regions, by the following circumstance. Regional experts will not often be involved in issues of a strategic nature due to highly centralised decision-making in those areas. For this reason, the perception of weak demand for strategic advice creates discomfort primarily for experts working in the capital city.

That aside, the survey showed that a majority of fairly typical representatives of the expert community believed that the authorities had a real interest, albeit selective and not very strong, in the use of their competencies. Turning now from the demand side, let us look at the supply side of the relationship between the authorities and experts.

In our survey, respondents were surprisingly open and critical in assessing the capacity and willingness of their colleagues to act as honest brokers. In particular, 80% of all those interviewed admitted that some experts were prepared intentionally and consciously to neglect some details or nuances of the picture in their judgements, as well as downplay the differences between firmly established facts and only partially confirmed hypotheses. Regarding the reasons for these kinds of biased judgements, 49% of respondents answered that this resulted from a desire to act in the interest of a specific client, while 39% explained it in terms of a desire to ensure support for a particular political orientation. Three more reasons – a desire to impose one's view of the world on the audience, a desire to portray oneself as more competent than one really was, and a desire to put one's point across in the most powerful and accessible way – were each shared by approximately 30% of the respondents. Finally, 19% were more straightforward and said that it could be explained simply by a desire to improve one's financial situation. The responses add up to more than 100%, since in some cases the respondents provided more than one answer. The same applies to the results reported in the tables below.

At first glance, opportunistic behaviour may look risky. Indeed, whilst offering advantages in the short run, it should seemingly in the long term have damaging reputational effects and result in those engaging in such behaviour losing out in what could be described as a form of natural selection. Yet, the survey data show this not to be the case, as can be seen in Table 2. In interpreting the data, we should not focus too much on how appropriate the opinions of most respondents about the success factors are; more important is that the views are widespread, hence serving as reference points for the coping behaviour of many experts. Apparently, experts perceive their field of activity as a competitive environment where success is determined by one's real skills and competences rather than by pure chance. At the same time, the experts who feel that it is their communication skills which are appreciated far outnumber those who believe in the importance of keeping their professional skills up to date, and even more so those who attach value to their integrity.

It could be hypothesised that an expert community ethos might provide a counter to external pressures. Respondents were therefore asked to estimate the extent to which experts are guided by the norms of an expert community. When asked to what extent expert community norms encouraged one to avoid giving insincere opinions, three respondent groups of roughly equal size (from 27% to 30%) selected the answers 'to a great extent', 'to a small extent' and 'do not encourage at all' (other respondents chose not to answer). Views on whether the norms encourage one to attach importance to having a scientific basis for one's statements were only a little better: 37% of survey respondents answered 'to a great extent', 43% said 'to a small extent' and 16% said 'do not encourage at all'. By contrast, the great majority of respondents were convinced that the community's norms encourage experts to offer persuasive opinions to their audience. Since persuasiveness is valued more than solid judgement, the ability to 'sell' an opinion which is not necessarily well-grounded is perceived quite positively. This was believed to be the case by 69% of respondents 'to a great extent', 27% agreed this only occurred 'to a small extent' and only 2% responded 'do not encourage at all'. Hence, the atmosphere in the expert community motivates experts to focus on external success factors rather than generate checks and balances that help resist temptations coming from the demand side.

The survey findings encourage us to take a closer look at whether Russian experts, including those well-known and influential, can be regarded as a single community. Only 13% of respondents agreed that there was an integrated community in Russia. In the opinion of 36% of respondents, boundaries separating experts were more significant than their unity, and 46% were convinced the boundaries were so significant that they ruled out the existence of a community. While 53% of respondents suggested the boundaries related to experts' political views, 44% highlighted the role of belonging to the same social circle and 34% emphasised the experience of working for the same clients. Less significant factors included belonging to the same school of thought, similar profession, university degree, level of skills, age, etc.

The picture becomes clearer when we turn to the responses relating to existing and desirable structures for funding expert activities. While statistical evidence about the shares of various sources of financing is not available, our respondents offered the following picture based on their extensive experience (the average values of respondents' estimates presented here should clearly be regarded as indicative). The share of contracts and grants directly from the authorities is 40%. Political structures and NGOs actively supporting the authorities account for another 16%. The estimated share of the private sector is 13%, and the share of research, educational and other politically neutral public sector organisations 12%. Further, the average share of funding coming from international and foreign funds is estimated at 7%, opposition political forces and organisations are estimated to give 6%, and the share of politically neutral Russian NGOs is estimated at 4%.

Most of the respondents claimed to want funding sources that have no direct interest in biased judgements to play a far stronger role in financing expert activities. This includes money from universities and research structures, and other public sector organisations and NGOs that represent the non-politicised part of civil society. In other words, on the one hand there is a perceptible desire for a resource base that would make expert activities as independent as possible, and on the other hand there is a clear understanding that reality is far from this ideal. Additionally, as shown previously, respondents recognise the great value of adjusting expert judgements to the interests of particular clients. Taken together, all these factors determine not just a shortage of totally neutral honest brokers, but also a systematic shift in the expert support for specific groups of interests in society at the expense of other groups. This can be seen in Table 3, which presents the distribution of answers to the question as to how often, in the respondent's view, experts give judgements that reflect the interests of particular social groups. Note that the survey question was not asking whether expert judgements reflect the interests of particular government bodies but rather the end beneficiaries of policy outcomes. Having said that, the results should not be taken as indicating that cooperation with the authorities influences expert judgements any less than cooperation with big business.

The comments above should not be taken as implying that, upon obtaining access to channels of influence on economic policy in general and on the budget process in particular, experts use them crudely for the benefit of their clients, much less that they are paid for direct lobbying. Such cases may occur but there is no evidence that they are widespread. Still, the above data convince us that a typical expert is constantly exposed to the 'magnetic field' of their own and third parties' interests. Due to this attraction, a consistent technocratic stance does not provide any competitive advantage over more flexible modes of behaviour, and in the long run the balance of interests does not lead to the position of an honest broker. Understandably, this compromises the capacity to meet the demand for honest brokers when such a demand is totally genuine.

Conclusion

The analysis undertaken in this article permits us to provide answers to the questions raised in the introduction. The first question relates to the authorities' demand for competent judgements and recommendations. The fact that the government has encouraged the establishment of numerous institutions that rely on expert knowledge in policy-making, including economic and budget policy, indicates that the demand for such knowledge is quite significant. However, it does not mean that the government is necessarily prepared to follow expert recommendations, even if they are perceived as valuable information that might bring a positive benefit if accepted. Having said that, it is unlikely that there is demand for inaccurate information. The conclusion, therefore, is that the authorities want to interact with competent professionals able to make a case for them, but that does not mean that they are looking for 'honest brokers' who will not sell something they do not believe in.

Our second question was about specific expert institutions and their activities in the broadly defined budget process. As shown above, these institutions generally do not intervene in the budget process in any serious way. When such interventions occur, they have little effect.

The answer to the third question derives from the results of the empirical research presented here. The research data have shown that experts tend not to present impartial judgements, in a way that would distinguish them from lobbyist groups. In other words, decision-makers may run the risk of facing the comfortable delusion which was referred to in the introduction. They might feel that they are receiving truly impartial advice, when they are not. Having said that, experts feel that what is required of them is servicing the routine work of various government institutions rather than playing a more independent role.

Finally, both the typical external environment of expert activity and the state of the expert community do not encourage competition in the provision of competent judgements. These factors are beneficial to those who are inclined to conform to the tastes and interests of their potential clients and the media. Overall, this explains the fairly weak and ineffective use of channels intended for expert participation in the budget process.

There is an obvious paradox: to a large extent, the reason why the government's demand for high quality expert activity is poorly accommodated is because there are no other potential demand agents able to act as a counterbalance to established experts. Interestingly, experts themselves express a clear need for such a counterbalance, at least with regards to funding. Another important circumstance that prevents a better response to the demand for competent and unbiased expert recommendations, both on the part of the government and the entire society, is the low level of self-organisation within the expert environment. Ultimately, the evolution of a real expert community with an appropriate ethos is an indispensable condition for bringing the attitudes of experts closer to the honest broker ideal.

Disclosure statement

No potential conflict of interest was reported by the author.

Funding

The study has been funded by the Russian Academic Excellence Project '5–100'.

References

Balayan, A., & Sungurov, A. (2016). *Fabriki mysli i ekspertnye soobshchestva* [Think factories and expert communities]. Saint-Petersburg: Aleteya.

Belyaeva, N. (2013). *Analiticheskiye soobshchestva v publichnoy politike: gtlobalny fenomen i rossiyskiye praktiki* [Analytical communities in public policy: A global phenomenon and Russian practices]. Moscow: ROSSPEN.

Belyaeva, N., Yena, O., Zaytsev, D., & Chulok, A. (2016). Otsenka vozdeystviya analiticheskikh soobshchestv na izmeneniya politiko-upravlencheskikh resheniy [Measuring the impact of analytical communities on changes in political and governance decisions]. *Public Administration Issues, 1*, 103–128.

Evans, Jr. A. B. (2008). The first steps of Russia's public chamber: Representation or coordination? *Demokratizatsiya: The Journal of Post-Soviet Democratization, 16*, 345–362.

Jakobson, L. (2008). Dialog grazhdanskogo obshchestva i vlasti: kachestvo interfeisa [The dialogue of civil society and authorities: The quality of interest]. In *Faktory razvitiya grazhdanskogo obshchestva i mehanismy ego vzaimodeistviya s gosudarstvom* [Factors of civil society development and mechanisms of its interaction with the state] (pp. 102–132). Moscow: Vershina.

Ledeneva, A. V. (2013). *Can Russia modernise? Sistema, power networks and informal governance*. Cambridge: Cambridge University Press.

Pielke, Jr. R. A. (2007). *The honest broker: Making sense of science in policy and politics*. Cambridge: Cambridge University Press.

Puetter, U. (2007). Providing venues for contestation: The role of expert committees and informal dialogue among ministers in European economic policy coordination. *Comparative European Politics, 5*, 18–35.

Rhodes, R. A. W. (1997). *Understanding governance: Policy networks, governance, reflexivity and accountability* (p. 235). Buckingham: Open University Press.

Rhodes, R. A. W. (2008). Executives in parliamentary government. In R. A. W. Rhodes, et al. (Eds.), *The Oxford handbook of political institutions* (pp. 323–343). Oxford: Oxford University Press.

Richter, J. (2009a). The ministry of civil society? The public chambers in the regions. *Problems of Post-Communism, 56*, 7–20.

Richter, J. (2009b). Putin and the public chamber. *Post-Soviet Affairs, 25*, 40–66.

Rutland, P. (in press). Russia's Post-Soviet Elite. In John Higley (Ed.), *The palgrave handbook of political elites*. http://prutland.faculty.wesleyan.edu/files/2016/07/post-soviet-elites.ed_.pdf

Sakwa, R. (2011). *Power and policy in Putin's Russia*. London: Routledge.

Stuvøy, K. (2014). Power and public chambers in the development of civil society in Russia. *Communist and Post-Communist Studies, 47*, 409–419.

Yakovlev, A. (2014). Russian modernization: Between the need for new players and the fear of losing control of rent sources. *Journal of Eurasian Studies, 5*, 10–20.

Yakovlev, A., Freinkman, L., Zolotov, A. (2016). Domestic and external factors in the development of Russia's economic think tanks sector. BOFIT Policy Brief, no.3. Helsinki: Bank of Finland.

Amending budget bills in the Russian State Duma

Ben Noble

ABSTRACT

Do budget bills change during review in the Russian State Duma? If so, by how much and why? Portrayals of the contemporary Federal Assembly as a 'rubber stamp' parliament would suggest that budget initiatives undergo no amendment during the formal period of legislative review. There is, however, evidence of bill change. The article's primary goal is to present this surprising evidence, focusing on changes to spending figures in the 2002–2016 budget bills. The article also discusses *why* such changes are made, assessing hypotheses concerning legislator influence, technical updating and intra-executive conflict.

Do budget bills change during review in the Russian State Duma? If so, by how much and why? Portrayals of the contemporary Federal Assembly as a 'rubber stamp' parliament would suggest that budget initiatives undergo no change during the formal period of legislative review. As Taylor (2014, p. 245) argues, 'although the Duma formally has the power to discuss and amend laws, its real function is simply to pass laws – it is not an opportunity for influence'. Indeed, commenting on current budgeting practices, Just Russia deputy Aleksandr Burkov has stated that 'parliament votes on budget expenditures, but no real discussion takes place' (cited in Dyatlovskaya, 2015).

There is, however, evidence of budget bill change. The article's primary goal is to present this surprising evidence, focusing on changes to spending figures, as well as other measures of amendment, for the period 2002–2016.[1] The article also discusses *why* such changes are made, assessing hypotheses concerning legislator influence, technical updating and intra-executive conflict.

The article consists of four sections. The first section provides a brief overview of the State Duma's place in the budget process. The second section then puts current practices in historical perspective, presenting data on budget scrutiny, 2002–2016. The third section – the core of the article – sets out and analyses data on budget bill amendments, discussing alternative explanations for these changes. Following a summary of the findings, the final section notes international parallels of Russian budget practices, as well as areas for future research.

The State Duma and the budget process

The passage of budget bills through the Federal Assembly is the final stage in the budget process before presidential signature into law. Although this stage is clearly associated with legislators, two points must be borne in mind: firstly, it is not the only stage during which parliamentarians are involved in budget discussions, as they are included – to varying degrees – in earlier discussions with executive actors; and, secondly, as will be made clear below, non-legislative actors – Government actors, most importantly – are active during the nominally legislative stage of the budgeting process. In light of these two points, we cannot infer actor *influence* simply from the *venue*, or stage, of budget policy-making.[2]

Consideration of the budget bill in the State Duma – the lower chamber of the federal parliament – is the most important phase of the parliamentary review process. Although Federation Council approval is required in order for an initiative to move on to the president, any consequential activity by senators takes place during the bill's review in the Duma. During Duma consideration, the bill is scrutinised by committees – according to policy area specialisation[3] – with the Budget Committee leading and coordinating this activity.[4] In order to progress through the lower chamber, budget initiatives need to pass Duma floor readings, the number and purpose of which have changed over time; but, overall, readings relate to particular features of bills, such as overall tax and spending figures, and, as a result, the size of the deficit, as well as particular figures for functional spending categories and sub-categories.

Russian budget bills over time – from chaos to control

Existing work on the parliamentary passage dynamics of Russian federal budgets relates primarily to the 1990s and early 2000s.[5] Contemporary practices, however, differ significantly. In contrast to the 'drawn-out, conflict-ridden budget cycle' (Chaisty, 2006, p. 161) in 1993, the 'procedural breakdown and deadlock' (Ostrow, 2000, p. 118) apparent in 1994 and 1995, and the production in 1997 of 'a budget that could not be implemented and which was not fulfilled until half-way through the year it was intended to cover' (Troxel, 2003, p. 159), the parliamentary passage of Russian budgets has become much less eventful. For example, whereas Russian budgets during the 1990s were often signed into law *after* the beginning of the planned fiscal year, this has not occurred since the 1999 budget. And, whereas Duma bill reading votes during the 1990s were often unpredictable – sometimes even resulting in failure – voting coalitions have become predictable, largely stable across readings and successful.[6]

This diachronic change in budget-passage dynamics is reflected in Figure 1, which presents data on the 2002–2016 budgets. The top graph presents budget bill velocities – that is, the number of days taken between Duma introduction and presidential signature. After relative stability from 2002 to 2006, the time spent by budget bills in the legislative process decreased roughly twofold by 2010. This suggests that the Duma spent less time scrutinising the Government's budget initiatives. However, bill velocity might not capture legislature-specific scrutiny. Various actors could be involved in the activities taking place during the legislative stage, and the time spent during this stage might not relate specifically to scrutiny. In response to this ambiguity, the middle graph presents a measure that should more closely track Duma scrutiny. Specifically, this measure is a proxy for the length of time budget bills are discussed in Duma plenary sessions.[7] The trend presented is congruent with the decline in bill velocity over time, although the change in floor activity is more than a twofold reduction, and the decline begins earlier.

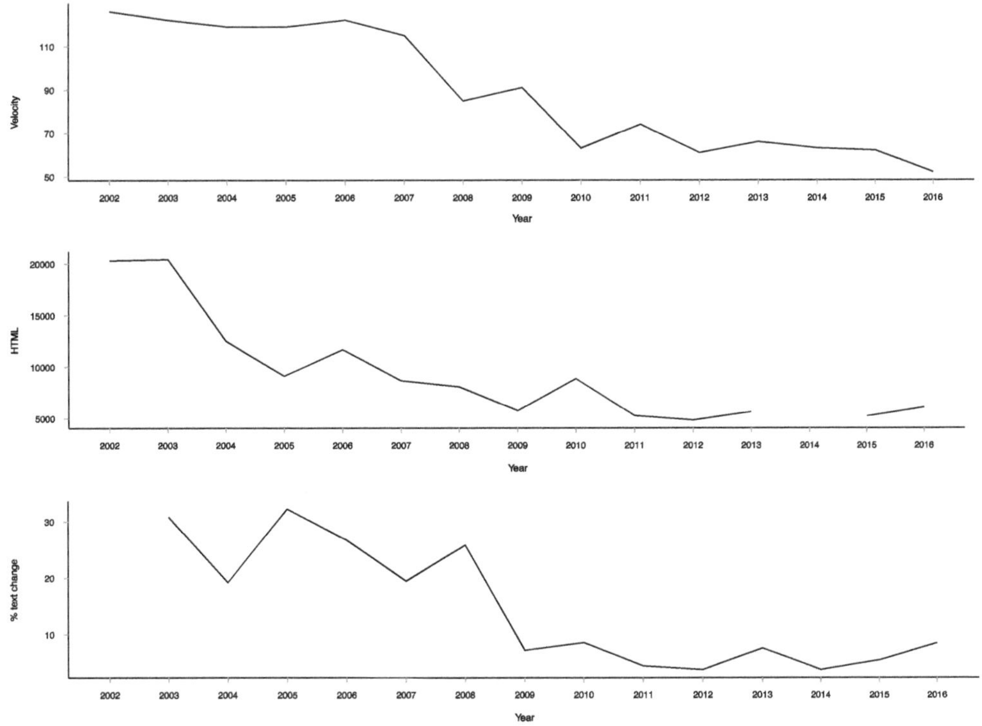

Figure 1. Measures of budget bill velocity, scrutiny and change, 2002–2016.
Notes: These data are taken from various sources: velocity information is taken from bill webpages (see the Appendix); HTML lines are taken from Duma floor transcripts hosted at http://transcript.duma.gov.ru; bill texts are taken from bill webpages; and law texts are taken from the *Zakonodatel'stvo Rossii* database (see the Appendix). The *y*-axes do not start at 0. The 2002 budget bill text is not available. Transcript data for the 2014 budget are incomplete.

The bottom graph in Figure 1 suggests, moreover, a relationship between this reduced Duma activity and the extent of change experienced by budget bills during legislative review. This graph presents a measure of text similarity between introduced bill and final law dyads for the 2002–2016 budgets.[8] The extent of budget bill amendment has reduced over time, with the sharpest drop experienced between the 2008 and 2009 budgets. The over-time trends displayed in these graphs are consistent with observations of increased Russian executive dominance over the legislature – also framed in terms of authoritarian backsliding – noted in existing scholarship (see, for example: Chaisty, 2012, 2013, 2014; Remington, 2013; Shul'man, 2013).

This executive dominance has also manifested itself in formal rule changes.[9] The time allowed for passage of the budget through the Duma has been reduced over time. The deadline for parliamentary introduction of the budget draft has shifted from 15 August (the original edition of the Budget Code),[10] to 26 August (116-FZ, 2000),[11] and to 1 October (216-FZ, 2010).[12] Moreover, for the 2015 and 2016 budgets, the deadline was shifted to 25 October (273-FZ, 2015)[13] and 1 November (158-FZ, 2016),[14] respectively, in response to the economic crisis.[15] In addition, amendments to the Budget Code introduced in 2007 (63-FZ) reduced the number of Duma readings of budget bills from four to three.[16] At the same time, the budget moved from a one-year to a three-year cycle. Thus, whereas all budgets up to and including the 2007 budget covered only the following fiscal year, budgets from 2008 have set out tax and spending plans for the following fiscal year, as well as two further 'planning' years.[17] Chaisty (2012, p. 97) attributes this shift to a three-year cycle to a desire 'to contain lobbying by United Russia deputies', characterising the formal changes as 'a major blow to the parliament's authority'.

Amendments and spending figures

The longitudinal picture of bill change presented in the lower graph of Figure 1 uses a measure of text change. Although this provides a preliminary picture of bill change over time, we should be more interested in the *substance* of change. In particular, do spending figures change during Duma review? Looking only at *overall*[18] budget expenditure figures in drafts and laws suggests there is little of interest to explain: from 2002 to 2016, these figures have changed only once during parliamentary consideration – for the 2002 budget. Whereas the version of the 2002 bill submitted by the Government to the Duma proposed a total expenditure of 1,871,871,050,000 roubles, the final law provided for 1,947,386,255,400.[19]

A different picture emerges, however, if we compare spending figures in bills and laws for *functional spending categories*, such as defence, healthcare and education. Although overall expenditure figures have not varied between bills and laws beginning with the 2003 budget, the *distribution* of spending across functional spending categories has changed every year during legislative review. In an analysis of budget amendments in the Japanese Diet, Meyer and Naka (1998, p. 274) calculate 'gross expenditure difference' as the sum of absolute 'budget-item-spending changes'. In effect, this measure sums the changes made to spending category figures, providing an overall statistic of amendment, but removing information on the *direction* of change. Figure 2 presents data on gross spending changes made during the Duma review of the 2002–2016 budget bills.

Two features stand out in Figure 2. Firstly, the 2002 budget is a clear outlier, showing a relatively high level of change. Indeed, as noted above, this was the last budget year to see a net difference between spending totals in the draft and the final law. The exceptional nature of the 2002 budget is consistent with changes in executive–legislative consultation practices. Beginning with the preparation of the 2003 budget in 2002, the Government held 'zero readings' – consultations between the Government and legislators *before* the budget draft's submission to the Duma and readings on the floor, with a view to incorporating policy preferences and constructing voting majorities (Shul'man, 2014, pp. 102–103; Svobodnaya analiticheskaya shkola, 2003). As a result, adjustments resulting from executive–legislative bargaining would more likely be made *before* legislative introduction from the 2003 budget onwards.[20] Secondly, although gross expenditure changes fell precipitously after 2002, change still occurred in later years. Why? The following will explore three possibilities, the first of which is that changes reflect legislator influence.

Legislator influence

Amendments made to budget initiatives during parliamentary passage are often attributed to legislator influence. According to Meyer and Naka (1998, p. 273; footnote 19), 'deviations in budgetary outcomes from proposals reflect the political power of the legislative and executive branch. The formulation of the budget can then be modelled as a bargaining process'. This strategic model is common in studies of the legislative stage of budgeting.

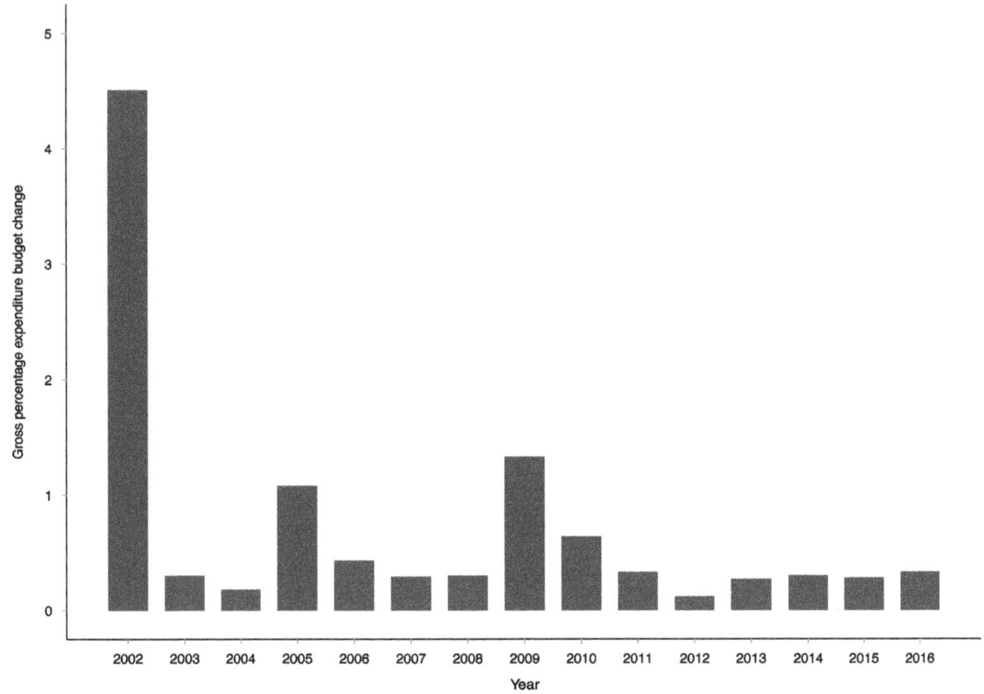

Figure 2. Gross percentage expenditure changes, 2002–2016.

Notes: Gross change percentages are calculated as follows: absolute values for category spending changes are summed; net overall expenditure change is then subtracted (only relevant for 2002); the resulting figure is then divided by two (given that expenditure changes balance to zero)[a] in order to avoid double counting; this figure is then added to net overall expenditure change (again, only making a difference in 2002); finally, this figure is expressed as a percentage of the overall expenditure presented in the budget draft.[b]

[a]Once overall tax and spending figures are adopted, subsequent changes to spending figures are matched – thus, an increase in one area of spending must be balanced by a decrease in another area. See article 201 of the Budget Code, available here: http://www.consultant.ru/document/cons_doc_LAW_19702/.

[b]For example, in 2004, the sum of absolute values for category spending changes comes to 9,368,283,800 roubles; there was no net overall expenditure change between the budget draft and law, so 0 is subtracted; the initial figure is divided by two; 0 is added; and the final figure, 4,684,141,900, is expressed as a percentage of draft overall expenditure, 2,659,447,000,000, which comes to 0.176%.

Araya (2015, p. 220), for example, argues that, '[w]hile the government has no motivations to amend its budget bill, the assembly is interested in adapting the budget to its preferences'. Similarly, in a study on US state budgeting, Clarke (1998, p. 12) uses as 'a measure of conflict between the governor and legislature, the percentage change made by the legislature to the governor's recommendation for each [executive] agency'. And Wehner (2010, p. 56) uses budgetary 'amendment activity' as a 'measure of [legislative] policy influence'.

One way to evaluate the hypothesis that parliamentarians are responsible for spending figure changes is to look at the *direction* of change. Are spending redistributions consistent with legislator – and, in turn, citizen – priorities? White (1982, pp. 84–87) uses this approach in his study of budget amendments introduced in the USSR Supreme Soviet. Finding

> evidence of a consistent attempt to increase the allocation of resources on categories of expenditure of obvious public appeal, such as socio-cultural purposes and the republics, rather than on others which may be of less immediate interest to local areas and constituents, such as administration, arms and the economy,

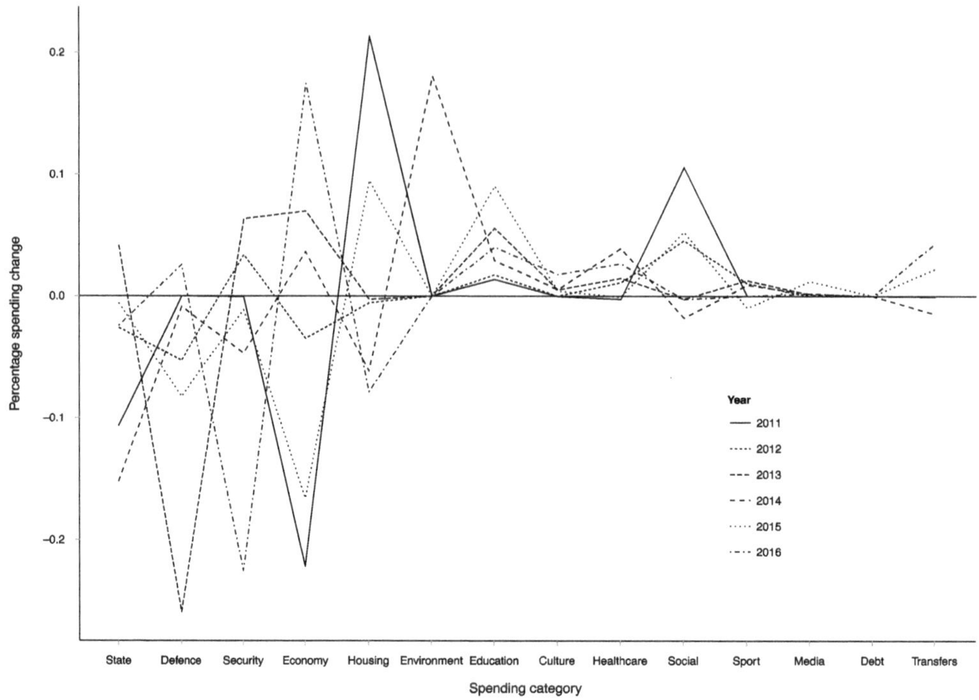

Figure 3. Percentage spending changes by budget category, 2011–2016.

White tentatively suggests that this might reflect 'an embryonic form of "linkage politics", connecting the mass public, deputies, the Supreme Soviet and the national budget' (1982, p. 87).[21] Working from this insight, Figure 3 presents changes to functional category spending figures during Duma review, expressed as a percentage of overall spending in the original version of budget bills, 2011–2016. These years are selected, given the stability of functional spending categories in this period.[22] Given the year-on-year variation, Figure 4 presents mean values for the six years.

Overall, the picture presented by Figures 3 and 4 bears a striking resemblance to White's (1982) findings: during legislative passage, spending is – on average – redistributed away from administration, defence, security and the economy to areas such as housing, education and social policy. Could it be that Duma deputies have been successful in amending budget bills, tailoring them more to their – and citizens' – preferences?

There are reasons to be cautious in interpreting these amendment data as clear-cut evidence of independent legislator influence. Firstly, the small number of observations available, as well as the variation displayed over these years, mean that we cannot speak of robust trends. Secondly, we have insufficient information regarding the divergent preferences of the Russian executive and Duma deputies in order to work back from observed category spending figure changes to actor influence. And, thirdly, even if these changes were consistent with clear estimations of actor preferences, this would not tell us *why* such changes were made to the budget bill. For example, rather than concessions granted to oppositional legislators, figure changes could be cosmetic amendments, granted to cultivate an image of executive magnanimity – or to help regime-loyal deputies to claim credit for spending beneficial to their nominal constituents.

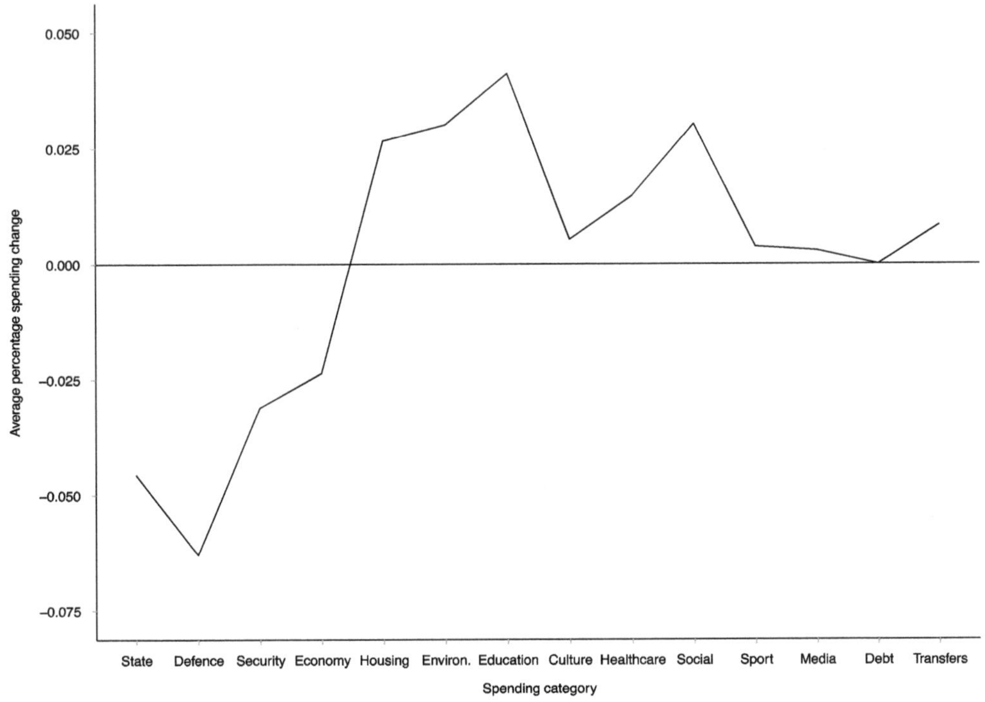

Figure 4. Mean percentage spending changes (pooled by year) across spending categories, 2011–2016.

Information on particular moved amendments should, however, help uncover the springs of change. Figure 5 presents a longitudinal picture of the raw number of amendments proposed and accepted for Russian budget bills, 2007–2016.[23] Overall, the trend is consistent with the diachronic data on bill text amendment presented in Figure 1: a reduction over time. But who is responsible for these particular amendments? Figure 6 presents data on the formal sponsorship of successful amendments, expressed as the percentage formally sponsored by the Government.

Figure 6 should make us even more cautious in attributing spending changes to legislator influence. Between the 2007 and 2009 budgets, although the raw number of amendments proposed reduced significantly, the proportion of successful amendments sponsored by the Government saw a more-than-twofold increase. Indeed, beginning with the 2008 budget, the majority of successful amendments have been sponsored by the Government: the mean proportion of successful budget amendments formally sponsored by the Government from 2008 to 2016 is around 82%. Furthermore, Government-sponsored amendments rarely fail: the mean success rate for the 2007–2016 budgets is 99%.[24] If we take this formal sponsorship information at face value, then amendatory activity in relation to Russian budget bills has become dominated by the executive.

At the same time, parliamentarians have been the formal sponsors of successful amendments, albeit in the minority. Moreover, these amendments make sense, insofar as there appears to be a clear link between the change made and actor interests. For example, a successful amendment to the 2013 budget sponsored by United Russia deputy Stanislav Govorukhin – a renowned Russian actor and director – introduced a change relating to Lenfil'm, one of the foremost film studios in Russia.[25] And a change to the 2014 budget

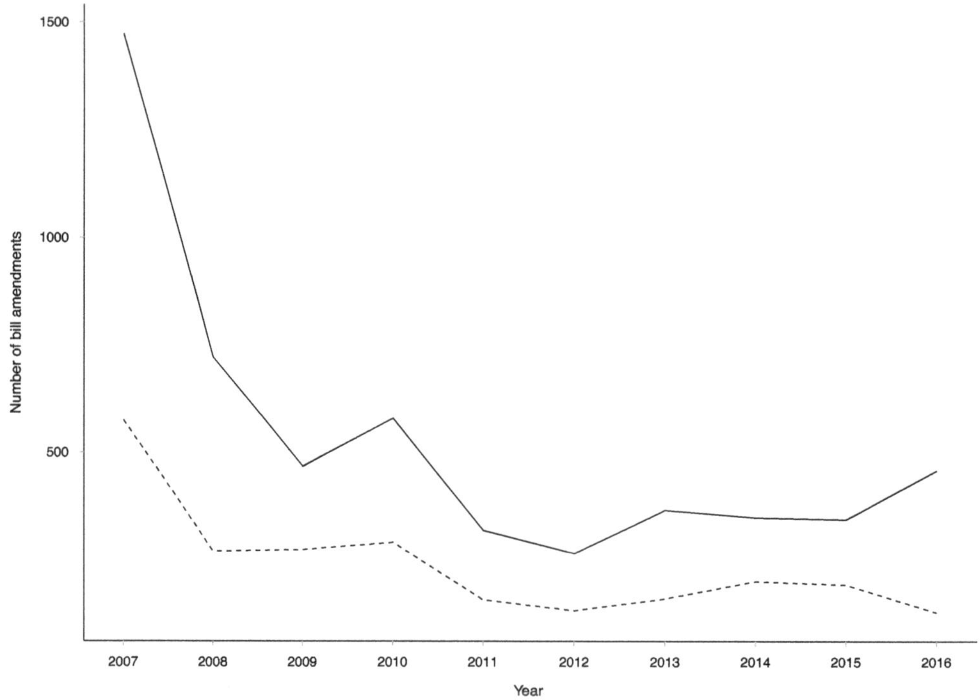

Figure 5. Number of bill amendments (moved and successful), 2007–2016.
Notes: The *y*-axis does not start at 0. The solid line relates to all proposed amendments; the dashed line to the total number of successful amendments. These data are taken from amendment tables (*tablitsy popravok*) produced by the Duma's Budget Committee in preparation for the budget bills' floor readings; they are available on the budget bills' webpages. Figures for successful amendments relate to committee decisions, rather than floor results. These numbers include all entries in particular amendment tables, ignoring finer distinctions between 'adopted' and 'partially adopted' or 'considered' amendments.

sponsored by senators Evgenii Bushmin, Sergei Riabukhin and Aleksandr Torshin provided funding for the Federation Council's television channel.[26] There is also evidence of success for *opposition*-sponsored amendments – for example, an amendment to the 2014 budget sponsored by KPRF deputies Gennadii Zyuganov, Nikolai Kolomeitsev and Oleg Kulikov increased healthcare spending.[27]

But this still leaves the majority of amendments to be explained: why would the Government want, or need, to modify its submitted budget bill? One possibility is consistent with the legislator influence hypothesis. In a study of budgeting in Sweden, Wehner (2013, p. 555) finds that some executive-sponsored budgetary changes 'responded to parliamentary demands'. Similarly, Baldez and Carey (2001, p. 123) report the 'selective ability of the executive to sponsor spending increases desired by legislators'; and Araya (2015, p. 217) argues somewhat more strongly that, '[a]s the government has no incentive to amend its budget bill, the executive amendments can be considered as concessions to Congress'. Alternatively, Huber (1996, pp. 157–158) demonstrates – in an analysis of budgeting in the French National Assembly, 1988–1989 – how executive actors can take credit for ideas originally expressed in legislator-sponsored amendments by repackaging them as government amendments.[28]

For the Russian case, however, there are reasons to question whether Government-sponsored amendments are, in fact, the result of legislator influence. Firstly, the inclusion of certain parliamentarians in pre-parliamentary discussions – including during budget draft

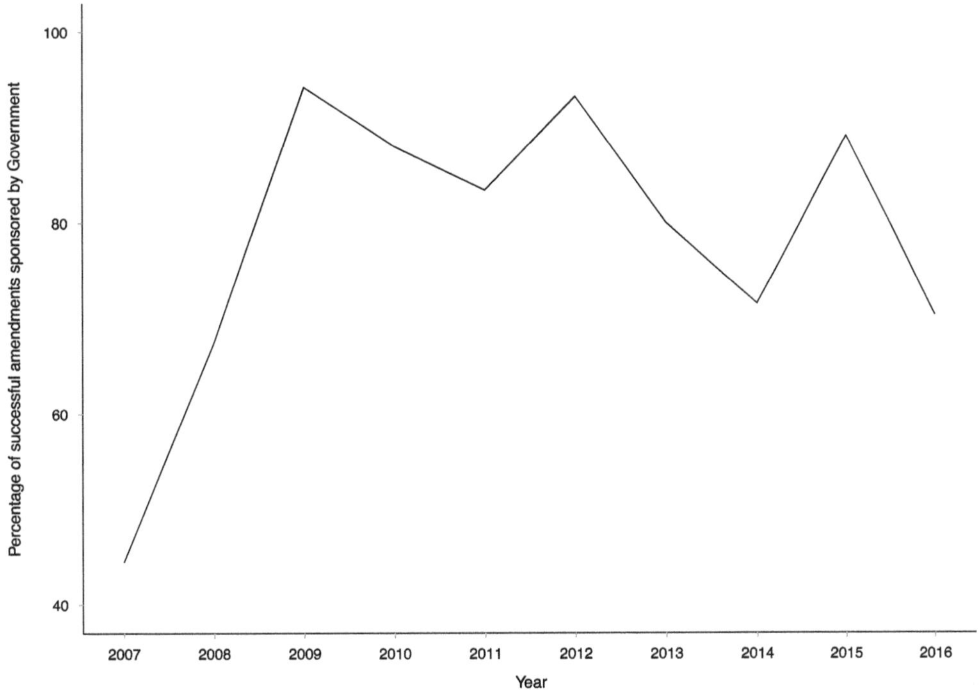

Figure 6. Percentage of successful amendments formally sponsored by the Government, 2007–2016.
Notes: The *y*-axis does not start at 0.

'zero readings' – should allow for the accommodation of legislator spending preferences earlier in the budgeting process.[29] Secondly, cooperation between parliamentarians and the Government is more manifestly exhibited by *co-sponsored* amendments by both actors, with, on average, around four such amendments moved for each of the 2007–2016 budget bills.[30] And thirdly, existing research suggests that mismatches between formal amendment sponsorship and actual authorship in Russia largely reflect the opposite situation: that Government-drafted changes are introduced by legislator proxies (see, for example, Chaisty, 2006, p. 130; and Noble, 2016a, 2016b). What, then, explains Government-sponsored changes to Government-drafted budget bills? We will now turn to two further explanations for bill amendments.

Technical updating

The budget bill might require technical updating, given revised economic data following bill introduction into the legislature. There is evidence of this beyond Russia. In Chile, for example, Baldez and Carey (2001, pp. 122–123) note that 'the executive proposal is originally submitted on October 1. During the next sixty days, as fourth-quarter tax receipts and economic projections take shape, the executive itself inevitably wants to make changes to fine tune its budget projections'. Similarly, Wehner (2013, p. 555) writes that executive amendments are sometimes the result of 'updated economic forecasts' in Sweden.

This need to tailor budget figures in response to changing socio-economic conditions and prognoses is reflected in supplementary budget bills in Russia, which are used to update the budget law during the fiscal year. For example, Federal Law 93 from 2015 reduced the 2015 budget's overall spending figure by around 300 billion roubles.[31] It is plausible that such changes might also need to be made following the introduction of the main budget bills, resulting in the redistribution of spending commitments. And there is evidence that such updating does, in fact, take place. For example, in the context of a worsening economic environment, President Putin signed a decree on 28 October 2014, requiring changes to salaries for officials of the Audit Chamber. As this decree was promulgated *after* the Government's introduction of its budget bill into the State Duma on 30 September, this salary change was inserted as a second-reading amendment to the budget initiative (Netreba, Milyukova, Bocharova, Dorokhov, & Sobolev, 2014).

Although such changes might be truly technical – not being the object of contestation between actors, that is – another plausible executive-centred account of budget bill amendments highlights the likelihood of *intra-executive* dispute. In brief, this explanation contends that budget changes reflect the resolution of intra-executive conflict over spending commitments, which spill over from pre-parliamentary, cabinet-level discussions.

Intra-executive spending disputes

Federal budget bills signed off by the Russian Government are not finalised documents. In theory, cabinet sign-off should signify that executive actors have reached their final positions on the details of budget bills. This comes at the end of a long and arduous decision-making process: draft macro-economic prognoses, and draft tax and spending policy documents, are circulated for discussion in spring, before discussion of budget parameters over the summer, and the draft budget is discussed by Government in the autumn.[32] However, there is evidence that intra-executive decision-making on the budget continues *after* cabinet sign-off. The following will present and discuss three types of evidence demonstrating that executive actors anticipate the continuation of decision-making at the point of bill sign-off; that decision-making does, in fact, continue; and that this has measurable effects on budget drafts following cabinet sign-off.[33]

In the formal decisions published following budget bill sign-off meetings, Government actors have been instructed to develop the respective bills. These instructions have been given for every budget bill for which data are available, excluding the 2010 budget.[34] This quite clearly puts paid to the notion that bill sign-off marks the end of intra-executive discussion. Take, for example, the 2014 budget. In the sign-off decision, the Minister of Finance Anton Siluanov and the Minister of Economic Development Aleksei Ulyukaev were instructed – along with 'interested federal organs of the executive' – to revise the draft bill. Executive actors were instructed to present this revised version to the Government on 23 September – albeit, crucially, *without* a further sign-off meeting with other executive actors – for subsequent introduction to the State Duma.[35]

The instruction for further development is, moreover, not merely a formality. Comments by executive actors themselves, as well as media reports, testify to the reality of post-sign-off discussions. For example, Butrin (2016) notes the continuation of inter-agency spending disputes, despite Government sign-off on the 2017 budget bill. And, for the same budget initiative, President Vladimir Putin noted that this post-sign-off conflict centred, in part, on differences between the Ministry of Finance and the Ministry of Economic Development regarding prognoses of Russia's socio-economic development (Latukhina, 2016).[36] What is more, these discussions result in meaningful changes to budget bill drafts. Between Government sign-off and Duma introduction, overall spending increased in the 2015 bill by around 30 billion roubles; by around 337 billion roubles for the 2016 budget bill; and by around 60 billion roubles for the 2017 bill.[37]

It is unlikely, moreover, that these spending figure changes made after Government sign-off, but before Duma introduction, constitute the end of the story. Comments made by Prime Minister Medvedev at the end of the 19 September 2013 Government sign-off meeting for the 2014 budget suggested anticipation of further development during *Duma* passage: 'After adopting these decisions, I once again draw attention to the need for consolidated work on the corresponding [budget] bill in the State Duma'.[38] Similarly, when commenting on the 2015 budget bill, Medvedev requested that Government actors 'present a unified position of the Government on the budget' during the bill's passage through the Duma.[39] The words 'consolidated' and 'unified' are instructive: both speak to the difficulties involved in reaching final, resolute decisions, as well as highlighting the difficulties of realising core executive control over executive actors during bill passage through the Duma. Ministries and agencies face the temptation of pursuing their own, individual spending preferences.

Dividing up finite resources between actors with conflicting spending priorities will always be tricky. There are particular reasons, however, why the Russian Government faces difficulties in reaching resolute budget spending decisions.[40] As with all executive decision-making, cabinet actors face limitations of time, resources and policy expertise when conducting policy decision-making (Martin & Vanberg, 2011). These limitations are exacerbated by the apparent reluctance of the Ministry of Finance to include external actors in pre-parliamentary budget decision-making (Prokopenko, 2016), which shifts inter-ministerial conflict resolution to later in the budgeting process.[41] Even when other actors take part in discussions – as, for example, when the Ministry of Economic Development and the Ministry of Finance have been tasked with revising the budget bill after cabinet sign-off – the absence of a formalised opportunity for *excluded* actors to sign off on these decisions means that parliamentary passage becomes an obvious opportunity for executive actors to challenge and attempt to modify the budget proposal.[42] Moreover, the presence of a disciplined majority of pro-executive Duma deputies removes, in a sense, the hard constraint of Government bill sign-off. Safe in the knowledge that a majority of deputies will ratify changes to Government-sponsored initiatives, intra-executive discussions can spill over into the nominally legislative stage of policy-making (see Noble, 2016a, 2016b).[43] As a result, although the legislative stage of the budget process is meant, in theory, to provide an opportunity for parliamentarians to review, critique and possibly amend budget proposals, this stage can also involve the resolution of intra-executive spending disputes.

Conclusion

Contrary to 'rubber stamp' expectations that the content of bills does not change during legislative review in contemporary Russia, this article demonstrates that budget bills do, in fact, undergo amendment during passage through the State Duma. Various measures of amendment were used above to demonstrate these changes, providing an unprecedented diachronic picture of budgeting in the Federal Assembly. The article also provides a preliminary assessment of the springs of this change, presenting evidence consistent with three hypotheses: legislator influence; technical updating; and intra-executive conflict. There are, it seems, various reasons for budget bill amendment – change is *equifinal*.[44]

One of the novel contributions of the article is its exploration of the hitherto largely unexplored *executive* springs of change. Intra-executive spending decision-making is not neatly contained in the pre-parliamentary stages of policy-making; the legislative passage of budget initiatives provides a final opportunity for executive actors to battle over the distribution of expenditures. This executive-centred account of budget bill amendments is not restricted to contemporary Russia. Writing of non-democratic Venezuela, Curristine and Bas (2007, p. 8) write that 'the majority of the amendments are actually proposed by the executive, reflecting its need to revise its original budget submission'. And, writing of the USSR, Hough and Fainsod (1979, p. 378) note that 'it is very probable that the preparatory committees [of the Supreme Soviet] are the place where final inter-agency agreement on the details of the plan and the budget are hammered out'.

Future work should both explore other possible sources of bill change, as well as attempt to specify the *proportion* of amendments resulting from different actors. What proportion of changes result from legislator – or, more broadly, non-executive – influence? How often are executive-inspired changes the object of contestation, rather than being merely technical adjustments to shifting socio-economic conditions? More broadly, answers to these questions will help track the State Duma's shifting place and role in Russian politics.

Notes

1. These years relate to the *fiscal* year, rather than the year of budget drafting, Duma consideration and legal promulgation. Thus, in what follows, 'the 2012 budget', for example, refers to the annual budget relating to the 2012 fiscal year, but considered by the Duma in 2011. In addition, even with the shift to the three-year budget cycle in Russia (discussed below), references in the text will refer to the first year and not the planning year – for example, 'the 2012 budget' refers to the bill or law 'On the Federal Budget for 2012 and the planning period 2013 and 2014'. Occasional references are made to budget bills outside of this timeframe.
2. As a result, this article does not attempt to answer a related, but broader, question: what influence does the State Duma, and deputies, have on the overall budget decision-making process?
3. See, for example, this list specifying which Duma committees were responsible for reviewing spending figures in different functional categories of the 2017 budget: http://asozd2.duma.gov.ru/main.nsf/(ViewDoc)?OpenAgent&work/dz.nsf/ByID&D917B4455A2C2F944325805A006294D7.
4. Expertise is also provided by the Audit Chamber, which produces a report (*zaklyuchenie*) on budget bills.
5. See, for example, Iwasaki (2002) and Sinel'nikov, Batkibekov, and Zolotareva (1999). Remington (2008) is an exception, providing a chapter-length commentary on Russian budget politics, although this includes data from a mixed time period. For example, data on the signing date and length of budgets are presented for 1992–2002, although the chapter also includes references to dynamics in the fourth Duma convocation (2004–2007). Chaisty (2012, p. 97) also provides a brief overview of budgeting changes during the 2000s.
6. By contrast, Ostrow (2000, p. 138) – writing of budgeting in the 1990s – remarks, '[w]hen budget votes are held in the Duma, no one has any idea what the outcome will be'.
7. The figures reported are the number of HTML lines of source code used to compose online transcripts of budget bill discussions on the Duma floor. Thus, the longer a bill is discussed on the floor, the more lines of text compose the official transcript, and the more HTML lines are needed to construct the webpage. As such, the measure is bounded on the left at 0 and unbounded on the right.

8. Specifically, the figures relate to percentage text change, focusing on unique word frequency differences – figures calculated according to the system proposed by Pedrazzani and Zucchini (2013) and using the JFreq programme (http://conjugateprior.org/software/jfreq/).
9. The rules governing legislative passage of the budget are located in various documents: the Constitution of the Russian Federation; the respective standing orders (*reglamenty*) of the State Duma, the Federation Council and the Government; and the Budget Code. These rules have changed over time. For example, the Budget Code has been amended more than 100 times since 2000. See the list of amendments at http://www.consultant.ru/popular/budget/.
10. The Budget Code is available here: http://www.consultant.ru/document/cons_doc_LAW_19702/.
11. The text of Federal Law 116 (2000) is available here: http://www.consultant.ru/document/cons_doc_LAW_28104/.
12. The text of Federal Law 216 (2010) is available here: http://www.consultant.ru/document/cons_doc_LAW_103029/.
13. The text of Federal Law 273 (2015) is available here: http://www.consultant.ru/document/cons_doc_LAW_186694/.
14. The text of Federal Law 158 (2016) is available here: http://www.consultant.ru/document/cons_doc_LAW_198846/.
15. Whereas previous editions of the Budget Code specified a particular number of days allowed for each stage (reading) of a bill's passage, a change in 2013 (104-FZ) means that the Duma has a total of 60 days to review the draft, with no constraint on how this time is apportioned. The text of Federal Law 104 (2013) is available here: http://www.consultant.ru/document/cons_doc_LAW_145985/.
16. The text of Federal Law 63 (2007) is available here: http://www.consultant.ru/document/cons_doc_LAW_58942/.
17. There have been exceptions, however. In response to the world financial crisis, the detailed portions of the 2010 budget covered only the following financial year, omitting detailed spending decisions for 2011 and 2012. In addition, the 2016 budget moved back to a one-year cycle, ostensibly as a result of the difficulties of planning during a period of economic volatility (see, for example, Filipenok, 2015). However, the Government announced in March 2016 that future budgets would return to the three-year cycle (see Butrin & Skorobogat'ko, 2016).
18. That is, the headline spending figures, which include both unclassified and classified spending figures.
19. This, therefore, contradicts a report from the Organisation for Economic Cooperation and Development (OECD) (Kraan, Bergvall, Hawkesworth, Kostyleva, & Witt, 2008, p. 30), which states that '[t]he totals of expenditures and revenues and the balance *have never* been changed in the final version of the budget law approved by the parliament as compared with the draft submitted to the State Duma' (emphasis added).
20. This point also serves to highlight that this article is focused on amendments made during the legislative passage of Russian budget bills, rather than the broader question of parliamentary influence on the wider budget process. An analysis of the latter question would require, for example, analysis of Duma involvement in pre-parliamentary, executive discussions, as well as oversight of budget implementation.
21. This is congruent with assumptions found in other, more recent works. For example, Miller (2015, p. 703) argues that 'increases in education and social welfare spending constitute general policy concessions, whereas increases in military spending indicate greater attention to satisfying elites'.
22. There were 14 separate spending categories for the 2011–2016 budgets. By contrast, there were 11 discrete categories during 2005–2010, and 27 categories for the 2002 and 2003 budgets.
23. Unfortunately, complete amendment data are only available on the Duma's online archive beginning with the 2007 budget.
24. Government amendments to the 2013 budget saw the lowest success rate, with 97.8% (the reasons for amendment failure are unknown); and amendments proposed by the Government to six other budget bills saw a 100% success rate.

25. See the amendment details in the committee amendment table here: http://asozd2.duma.gov.ru/main.nsf/(ViewDoc)?OpenAgent&work/dz.nsf/ByID&C9F279539EDBCC0143257AB6007EE8FF.
26. See the amendment details in the committee amendment table here: http://asozd2.duma.gov.ru/main.nsf/(ViewDoc)?OpenAgent&work/dz.nsf/ByID&58B022C1862D4DE943257C2800033140.
27. See the amendment details in the committee amendment table here: http://asozd2.duma.gov.ru/main.nsf/(ViewDoc)?OpenAgent&work/dz.nsf/ByID&1723B39E90B8551143257C280002FC32.
28. One broader implication of these findings, of course, is that *formal* sponsorship information cannot provide a reliable guide to the *actual* agents of change or the ideational sources of amendments.
29. That being said, we have very little information concerning the actors included in these discussions, as well as the extent to which the negotiations are efficient in reconciling executive and legislative preferences on spending commitments. For budgeting in the third Duma convocation, Iwasaki (2002, pp. 309–310) reports that issues remained unresolved following 'zero readings', meaning that the Federal Assembly's discussion occupied 'a very important position in the budget compilation'. However, this relates to a period of markedly different executive–legislative relations. It is plausible to assume that, when pre-parliamentary executive–legislative discussions now take place, issues raised are resolved more effectively.
30. Specifically, for these 10 budget bills, co-sponsored amendments numbered 9, 2, 0, 21, 1, 2, 4, 0, 0 and 0, respectively. These numbers are drawn from the committee amendment tables on the bills' webpages.
31. The text of Federal Law 93 (2015) is available here: http://www.consultant.ru/document/cons_doc_LAW_178391/.
32. See the article by Stephen Fortescue in this special issue for details of the pre-parliamentary, executive stage of the budgeting process.
33. This evidence involves partial transcripts of Government meetings, made available on the Government's official website. There are, clearly, reasons to be cautious when using this information. As an incomplete and public record, it is unclear which portions of discussion are not made available; and actors are, no doubt, fully aware of the strategic considerations necessary when discussing policy matters in public. As a result, this information cannot be taken as a faithful record of intra-executive relations.
34. These formal decisions are available on the Government's website: http://government.ru/meetings/.
35. The formal decision is available here: http://government.ru/meetings/5830/decisions/.
36. See also Prokopenko and Bazanova (2015).
37. Budget drafts signed off on by the Government are hosted on the website http://regulation.gov.ru/.
38. A transcript of Medvedev's public comments during the Government meeting are available here: http://government.ru/meetings/5830/stenograms/.
39. A transcript of Medvedev's public comments during the Government meeting are available here: http://government.ru/meetings/14808/stenograms/.
40. Indeed, these difficulties associated with intra-executive decision-making are, no doubt, compounded during periods of economic crisis, during which socio-economic conditions are volatile, economic prognoses are uncertain and there are manifest pressures on resource distribution.
41. In addition, the possibility of presidential intervention in decision-making – as noted above – likely weakens the incentives for inter-ministerial cooperation, as well as the likelihood of core executive control (see Fortescue, 2012).
42. On the sign-off (*soglasovanie*) process more generally, see Fortescue (2010).
43. It might be argued that reputational concerns regarding the airing of the executive's dirty laundry in the relative publicity of parliament would prevent the spill-over of intra-executive conflict into the Duma. And yet, although intra-executive conflict resolution might occur during the *stage* of parliamentary review, it will be unlikely to take place in the relative publicity of parliament itself.

44. For discussions of equifinality, see George and Bennett (2005, pp. 161, 215) and Haggard and Kaufman (2012, p. 498).
45. This is the website address: http://asozd2.duma.gov.ru/.
46. Budget bill webpages, 2002–2016: 2002 http://asozd2.duma.gov.ru/main.nsf/(Spravka)?OpenAgent&RN=125501-3; 2003 http://asozd2.duma.gov.ru/main.nsf/(Spravka)?OpenAgent&RN=235269-3; 2004 http://asozd2.duma.gov.ru/main.nsf/(Spravka)?OpenAgent&RN=362797-3; 2005 http://asozd2.duma.gov.ru/main.nsf/(Spravka)?OpenAgent&RN=86859-4; 2006 http://asozd2.duma.gov.ru/main.nsf/(Spravka)?OpenAgent&RN=211446-4; 2007 http://asozd2.duma.gov.ru/main.nsf/(Spravka)?OpenAgent&RN=335233-4; 2008 http://asozd2.duma.gov.ru/main.nsf/(Spravka)?OpenAgent&RN=425229-4; 2009 http://asozd2.duma.gov.ru/main.nsf/(Spravka)?OpenAgent&RN=94777-5; 2010 http://asozd2.duma.gov.ru/main.nsf/(Spravka)?OpenAgent&RN=258591-5; 2011 http://asozd2.duma.gov.ru/main.nsf/(Spravka)?OpenAgent&RN=433091-5; 2012 http://asozd2.duma.gov.ru/main.nsf/(Spravka)?OpenAgent&RN=607158-5; 2013 http://asozd2.duma.gov.ru/main.nsf/(Spravka)?OpenAgent&RN=143344-6; 2014 http://asozd2.duma.gov.ru/main.nsf/(Spravka)?OpenAgent&RN=348499-6; 2015 http://asozd2.duma.gov.ru/main.nsf/(Spravka)?OpenAgent&RN=611445-6; 2016 http://asozd2.duma.gov.ru/main.nsf/(Spravka)?OpenAgent&RN=911755-6.
47. These documents are hosted here: http://www.budgetrf.ru/Publications/Schpalata/Zakluchenia/schpalzakluch_index.htm.
48. Cooper (2007, p. 2) argues that, '[b]y dropping the usual appendix providing a functional breakdown of total budget expenditure, an unprecedented degree of classification of the budget has been achieved, in addition to the traditional practice of declaring some appendix secret'.
49. This is the website address: http://pravo.gov.ru/ips.html.
50. The reports are available here: http://www.roskazna.ru/ispolnenie-byudzhetov/.
51. The former reports are available on the following webpages, relating to the main supplementary budget bills, for particular budget years: 2008 http://asozd2.duma.gov.ru/main.nsf/(Spravka)?OpenAgent&RN=67230-5; 2009 http://asozd2.duma.gov.ru/main.nsf/(Spravka)?OpenAgent&RN=181653-5; 2011 http://asozd2.duma.gov.ru/main.nsf/(Spravka)?OpenAgent&RN=542807-5. The latter reports are available here: http://audit.gov.ru/activities/audit-of-the-federal-budget/.
52. The report is available here: http://asozd2.duma.gov.ru/main.nsf/(ViewDoc)?OpenAgent&arhiv/a_dz_5.nsf/ByID&4ABCC02BC3655D37C325767B002FD086.

Acknowledgements

Thanks to Fabian Burkhardt, Julian Cooper, Stephen Fortescue, Lev Jakobson, Marina Khmelnitskaya and Peter Rutland for feedback.

Disclosure statement

No potential conflict of interest was reported by the author.

ORCID

Ben Noble http://orcid.org/0000-0002-6844-8886

References

Araya, I. (2015). Budgetary negotiations: How the Chilean Congress overcomes its constitutional limitations. *The Journal of Legislative Studies, 21*, 213–231.

Baldez, L., & Carey, J. (2001). Budget procedure and fiscal restraint in posttransition Chile. In S. Haggard & M. McCubbins (Eds.), *Presidents, parliaments, and policy* (pp. 105–148). Cambridge: Cambridge University Press.

Butrin, D. (2016, October 21). Byudzhet nedolechen [The budget has not been fully cured]. *Kommersant*. Retrieved November 9, 2016, from http://kommersant.ru/doc/3121163?utm_source=kommersant&utm_medium=economic&utm_campaign=four.

Butrin, D., & Skorobogat'ko, D. (2016, March 16). Novaya byudzhetnaya normal'nost [The new budgetary normal]. *Kommersant*. Retrieved November 9, 2016, from http://kommersant.ru/doc/2938616.

Chaisty, P. (2006). *Legislative politics and economic power in Russia*. Basingstoke; New York, NY: Palgrave Macmillan.

Chaisty, P. (2012). The Federal Assembly and the power vertical. In G. Gill & J. Young (Eds.), *Routledge handbook of Russian politics and society* (pp. 92–101). Abingdon; New York, NY: Routledge.

Chaisty, P. (2013). The preponderance and effects of sectoral ties in the State Duma. *Europe- Asia Studies, 65*, 717–736.

Chaisty, P. (2014). Presidential dynamics and legislative velocity in Russia, 1994–2007. *East European Politics, 30*, 588–601.

Clarke, W. (1998). Divided government and budget conflict in the US states. *Legislative Studies Quarterly, 23*, 5–22.

Cooper, J. (2007). *Military expenditure in the three-year federal budget of the Russian Federation, 2008–10*. Retrieved November 20, 2016, from http://kms2.isn.ethz.ch/serviceengine/Files/ESDP/96405/ipublicationdocument_singledocument/be712761-0db9-4536-ba5e-49cde3c19695/en/2007_10_cooper20071010%5B1%5D.pdf.

Cooper, J. (2013). *Russian military expenditure: Data, analysis and issues*. FOI (Swedish Defence Research Agency) Report (Report No. FOI-R-3688-SE). Retrieved October 1, 2015, from http://www.foi.se/Documents/foir_3688.pdf.

Curristine, T., & Bas, M. (2007). Budgeting in Latin America. *OECD Journal on Budgeting, 7*(1), 1–37.

Dyatlovskaya, E. (2015, October 28). A sud'i kto? [Who are the judges?]. *Novye izvestiya*. Retrieved November 9, 2016, from http://www.newizv.ru/politics/2015-10-28/229683-a-sudi-kto.html#.VjDA98Gm1kA.

Filipenok, A. (2015, September 1). Pravitel'stvo namereno otkazat'sya ot "byudzheta dolgosrochnoi ustoichivosti"[TheGovernmentintendstoabandona"budgetoflong-termstability"].*RBKDaily*.Retrieved November 9, 2016, from http://top.rbc.ru/economics/01/09/2015/55e511299a7947b32688d438.

Fortescue, S. (2010). Institutionalisation and personalism in the policy-making process of the Soviet Union and post-Soviet Russia. In S. Fortescue (Ed.), *Russian politics from Lenin to Putin* (pp. 21–50). Basingstoke: Palgrave Macmillan.

Fortescue, S. (2012). The policymaking process in Putin's prime ministership. In L. Jonson & S. White (Eds.), *Waiting for reform under Putin and Medvedev* (pp. 119–139). Basingstoke: Palgrave Macmillan.

George, A., & Bennett, A. (2005). *Case studies and theory development in the social sciences*. Cambridge, MA: MIT Press.

Haggard, S., & Kaufman, R. (2012). Inequality and regime change: Democratic transitions and the stability of democratic rule. *American Political Science Review, 106*, 495–516.

Hough, J., & Fainsod, M. (1979). *How the Soviet Union is governed*. Cambridge, MA: Harvard University Press.

Huber, J. (1996). *Rationalizing parliament: Legislative institutions and party politics in France*. Cambridge: Cambridge University Press.

Iwasaki, I. (2002). The State budget compilation process in Russia: Institutional framework and practice. *Post-Communist Economies, 14*, 301–319.

Kraan, D., Bergvall, D., Hawkesworth, I., Kostyleva, V., & Witt, M. (2008). Budgeting in Russia. *OECD Journal on Budgeting, 8*(2), 1–58.

Latukhina, K. (2016, October 25). Putin obsudil s Medvedevym sotsial'nye obyazatel'stva [Putin discussed social obligations with Medvedev]. *Rossiiskaya gazeta*. Retrieved November 9, 2016, from https://rg.ru/2016/10/25/putin-obsudil-s-medvedevym-socialnye-obiazatelstva.html.

Martin, L., & Vanberg, G. (2011). *Parliaments and coalitions: The role of legislative institutions in multiparty governance*. Oxford: Oxford University Press.

Meyer, S., & Naka, S. (1998). Legislative influences in Japanese budgetary politics. *Public Choice, 94*, 267–288.

Miller, M. (2015). Elections, information, and policy responsiveness in autocratic regimes. *Comparative Political Studies, 48*, 691–727.

Netreba, P., Milyukova, Y., Bocharova, S., Dorokhov, R., & Sobolev, S. (2014, November 10). Pravitel'stvo nashlo dopolnitel'nye den'gi na Schetnuyu palatu i ChM-2018 [The Government has found additional money for the Audit Chamber and the World Cup 2018]. *RBK Daily*. Retrieved November 9, 2016, from http://top.rbc.ru/economics/10/11/2014/545cd636cbb20f112dfcb197.

Noble, B. (2016a). *Rethinking 'rubber stamps': Legislative subservience, executive factionalism, and policy-making in the Russian State Duma*. DPhil dissertation, University of Oxford.

Noble, B. (2016b). *Authoritarian legislatures, policy-making, and intra-executive constraints*. Paper presented at the 2016 annual conference of the Midwest Political Science Association, Chicago.

Ostrow, J. (2000). *Comparing post-Soviet legislatures: A theory of institutional design and political conflict*. Columbus, OH: Ohio State University Press.

Pedrazzani, A., & Zucchini, F. (2013). Horses and hippos: Why Italian government bills change in the legislative arena, 1987–2006. *European Journal of Political Research, 52*, 687–714.

Prokopenko, A. (2016, October 19). Novye pravila byudzheta [New rules of the budget]. *Vedomosti*. Retrieved November 17, 2016, from http://www.vedomosti.ru/opinion/articles/2016/10/19/661524-novie-pravila.

Prokopenko, A., & Bazanova, E. (2015, October 13). Byudzhet opyat' ne soshelsya s makroprognozom [The budget once again did not converge with the macro-prognosis]. *Vedomosti*. Retrieved November 9, 2016, from http://www.vedomosti.ru/economics/articles/2016/10/12/660725-byudzhet-makroprognozom.

Remington, T. (2008). Separation of powers and legislative oversight in Russia. In R. Stapenhurst, R. Pelizzo, D. Olson, & L. von Trapp (Eds.), *Legislative oversight and budgeting: A world perspective* (pp. 173–182). Washington, DC: The World Bank.

Remington, T. (2013). Parliament and the dominant party regime. In S. Wegren (Ed.), *Return to Putin's Russia: Past imperfect, future uncertain* (pp. 45–62). Plymouth; Lanham, MD: Rowman and Littlefield.

Shul'man, E. (2013). *Politicheskie usloviya i faktory transformatsii zakonotvorcheskogo protsessa v sovremennoi Rossii* [The political conditions and factors of the transformation of the law-making process in contemporary Russia]. PhD dissertation, Russian Academy of National Economy and State Service, Moscow.

Shul'man, E. (2014). *Zakonotvorchestvo kak politicheskii protsess* [Law-making as a political process]. Moscow: Moskovskaya shkola grazhdanskogo prosveshcheniya.

Sinel'nikov, S., Batkibekov, S., & Zolotareva, A. (1999). Zakonodatel'nye i politicheskie aspekty byudzhetnoi politiki v postsovetskoi Rossii [Legal and political aspects of budget policy in post-Soviet Russia]. Retrieved November 9, 2016, from http://www.iep.ru/files/persona/sinelnikov/budpol.pdf

Svobodnaya analiticheskaya shkola. (2003). *Kommentarii k federal'nomu byudzhetu 2002-2003*. Moscow. Retrieved November 9, 2016, from http://www.budgetrf.ru/Publications/Analysis/sash/an_sash_08092003/an_sash_08092003020.htm.

Taylor, B. (2014). Police reform in Russia: The policy process in a hybrid regime. *Post-Soviet Affairs, 30*, 226–255.

Troxel, T. (2003). *Parliamentary power in Russia, 1994–2001: President vs. parliament*. Basingstoke; New York, NY: Palgrave Macmillan.

Wehner, J. (2010). *Legislatures and the budget process: The myth of fiscal control*. Basingstoke; New York, NY: Palgrave Macmillan.

Wehner, J. (2013). Electoral budget cycles in legislatures. *Legislative Studies Quarterly, 38*, 545–570.

White, S. (1982). The Supreme Soviet and budgetary politics in the USSR. *British Journal of Political Science, 12*, 75–94.

Zatsepin, V. 2014. *Laws, secrecy and statistics: Recent developments in Russian defence budgeting*. Paper presented at the Forum for Economists International conference, Amsterdam, May-June. Retrieved October 1, 2015, from http://www.iep.ru/files/news/zatsepin_text_01.06.14.pdf.

Appendix 1. Data sources

1. Budget bills

a. Texts

Budget bill texts are available on the Duma's legislative information website, ASOZD,[45] beginning with the 2003 budget.[46] Unfortunately, digital versions of bill texts are not available before this budget year.

b. 1. Overall category spending totals

For 2002–2004, draft overall category spending figures have been collated from reports compiled by the Russian Audit Chamber on budget drafts.[47] The relevant appendix is available on budget bill webpages for the 2005, 2006 and 2007 budgets. Beginning with the 2008 budget, the Government ceased making the relevant appendix public.[48] Fortunately, however, approximate overall category spending figures are included in the Ministry of Finance's explanatory notes on the introduced budget bills and are available on bill webpages.

2. Budget laws

a. Texts

Original versions of budget law texts – that is, versions not amended by the passage of later laws – are available on the legal information portal *Zakonodatel'stvo Rossii*[49] – an official resource curated by the Federal Protection Service, *Federal'naia sluzhba okhrany*.

b. 2. Overall category spending figures

From the 2002 budget to the 2007 budget, appendices outlining final overall spending category figures are available as appendices to the main budget text. These appendices are available on bill webpages. However, as with the same information for budget bills, these figures have not been made public beginning with the 2008 budget. We need, therefore, another source for these overall figures. Both Cooper (2013, p. 31) and Zatsepin (2014, p. 91) cite budget implementation reports (monthly, quarterly and yearly) produced by the Federal Exchequer (*Federal'noe kaznacheistvo*) as a source of information on final expenditure levels. These reports provide the needed information for the 2012–2016 budgets.[50] Figures cited for the 2008, 2009, 2010 and 2011 budgets, however, relate only to unclassified spending and/or provide figures that incorporate subsequent amendments. Fortunately, the Audit Chamber produces a report – *Zaklyuchnie Schetnoi palaty Rossiiskoi Federatsii na proekt federal'nogo zakona* – on supplementary budget bills, as well as a report on the implementation of the budget – *Zaklyuchenie Schetnoi palaty Rossiiskoi Federatsii na otchet ob ispolnenii federal'nogo byudzheta*. These reports contain information on expenditure category totals from the original, unamended budget laws for the 2008, 2009 and 2011 budgets.[51] For 2010, the Federation Council's Budget Committee fortunately included final overall category spending figures in its report (*zaklyuchenie*).[52] It is not clear either why the Audit Chamber or the Federation Council are able to make these figures public when it appears that the Government has gone to some lengths to prevent the publication of these spending data.

The role of the executive in Russian budget formation

Stephen Fortescue

ABSTRACT
The article provides an examination of the role of Russia's dual (semi-presidential) executive in the budget process. The Constitution gives the president a strategic role, leaving operational budget formation to the 'government', chaired by the prime minister, whereas the common view of Russian policy making is of the president's 'hands-on management'. The article looks at how the president engages in the budget process, and whether, on the one hand, excessive 'hands-on' presidential involvement leads to a disrupted policy process, or, on the other hand, it breaks down the inter-agency deadlocks that are common in Russian policy making. The conclusion is that a reasonable balance is found between the two.

In previous accounts of Russian executive policy making this author has painted a mixed picture, both in terms of process and outcomes: of a general willingness to address issues requiring attention, resulting sometimes in rapid and decisive action, but often in a very drawn-out process with heavily compromised outcomes (Fortescue, 2012, pp. 121–123).

An important reason for the mixed picture is almost certainly the role played by the president in each particular case. If Vladimir Putin is highly committed to a particular policy outcome he has the formal and informal power to get what he wants with the minimum of fuss and process (the question then becoming whether what he wants is wise and whether any doubts on that score arise because a lack of fuss and process has meant a lack of input from a sufficient range of informed actors) (Fortescue, 2017). If Putin has a less direct personal commitment, the policy process struggles to arrive at a clear and quick outcome.

The question then becomes why in a large and complex society with well-established and elaborate bureaucratic structures and processes it takes the personal commitment of one person to achieve decisive outcomes. One can refer in general terms to a Russian cultural tradition of deference to a single Tsar-like leader, a tradition which it could be said Putin has done little to undermine. But without dismissing such a broad explanation, one would like to go beyond it and find more precise structural and procedural explanations.

The Russian Constitution is semi-presidential, that is, it gives the president a strategic, not operational role, particularly in socio-economic affairs. The actual running of socio-economic affairs is left to what in Russian is called 'the government' (*pravitel'stvo*), that is, ministries and equivalent agencies under the command of a prime minister.[1] The prime minister is not seen as having a strategic role, and indeed tends to be – by the nature of the relationship with the president – not just a subordinate figure but usually a weak one. The ministries, at least partly as a consequence, tend to be what could be called 'technocratic'. They see their role as to pursue the interests implied in their functional responsibilities, and they are usually headed by someone possessing the specialised knowledge required of that functional role. The system has traditionally had strong processes of consultation and sign off (*soglasovanie*) to ensure that the technocratic interests of the ministries are heard and responded to (Fortescue, 2016, p. 428).

Technocratic ministries and a weak prime minister are enough in themselves to produce drawn-out, lowest common denominator policy making. To overcome it the president comes under pressure to become operationally involved, to engage in so-called *ruchnoe upravlenie* (hands-on management). Indeed he is pressured into becoming involved a lot more than he wants and can efficiently manage. As established procedures become compromised and policy making more ad hoc and even chaotic, participants have less and less respect for both process and outcomes, to the point of what this author, and Tat'iana Stanovaia, have called 'policy irresponsibility' (Fortescue, 2016, p. 444; Stanovaia, 2014).

In this article the author asks whether this description can be applied to the budget policy process. Is budget formation something in which the president has played a strategic role, leaving the operational process to the government? If not, has his intervention in the operational process led to 'policy irresponsibility'?[2]

The Constitution

Article 3 of the Constitution states:

> The President of the Russian Federation in accordance with the Constitution of the Russian Federation and federal laws sets the basic directions of the domestic and foreign policy of the state.

The Constitution does not say any more on the president's powers in domestic policy, whereas it states explicitly the responsibility of the government for budget formation.[3] As Prime Minister Medvedev put it at a budget planning meeting in 2015, preparing the budget 'is the main responsibility of the government' (government.ru/news/18603/).

Putin gives voice to his 'setting of the basic directions' of economic and budget policy in a great variety of forums, including set-piece speeches at international forums, interviews and on-line Q&A events, and semi-formal occasions such as addressing ceremonial meetings of the collegiums of key ministries. As something of a one-off, for his third presidential campaign in 2012 he presented in a number of newspaper articles a detailed and expensive set of targets across a number of policy areas, in particular social policy. They were then formalised as policy directives in the famous 'May decrees' once he assumed the presidency. They have played a major role in budget formation ever since.

Formally the most important presidential forum is the *Poslanie* (Address), roughly equivalent to the State of the Union address of the US President. In 2014 the Budget Address, once separate, was folded into the general Address. This was a change of some significance, since the Budget Address was usually delivered in June, after the early stages of budget formation had already begun.[4] The combined Address is delivered in December, well before the budget preparation cycle gets underway in about April. While ensuring that the president is able to set out his budget priorities early, the new arrangement also means that by the time the budget to which the Address is directed comes to be implemented – more than a year later – circumstances may have changed significantly.

The Address sets out Putin's priorities of the time, sometimes quite specifically. Thus the Address of 2014, after a lot of aggressively patriotic rhetoric, said the following on budget policy:

> The quality and size of the Russian economy must match our geopolitical and historical role. We must escape from the trap of zero growth rates and in the space of three to four years achieve a growth rate higher than the global average. Only thus can we increase Russia's share in the global economy and thereby strengthen our influence and economic independence. ... It is important to maintain a stable macroeconomic situation, reducing the medium-term outlook for inflation to 4%, but without, I emphasise, dampening business activity. We must finally learn how to harmoniously combine two goals: restrain inflation and stimulate growth (news.kremlin.ru/news/47173/).

In April the following year, as the budget was being drawn up, Putin acknowledged that difficult circumstances necessitated flexibility, but that he did not want the guidelines (*orientiry*) set out in the Address – in terms of both growth and macroeconomic stability – forgotten (kremlin.ru/events/president/news/49052). Brief reference will be made to aspects of the most recent 2016 Address later in this article.

Putin's budget priorities

The guidelines in Putin's 2014 Address sum up his core budget policy orientations reasonably well, although further details are required. But first something speculative on where he might get his ideas from. Presumably his own thoughts and experiences lay a foundation.[5] They are likely to be developed or reinforced by informal discussions with close friends. They are believed mostly to be so-called *siloviki*, with backgrounds and current positions in the security agencies and robust views on Russia's place on the world and the need to spend money to achieve it. But it is widely acknowledged that someone with a very different view of matters of government policy, Aleksei Kudrin, his long-serving Minister of Finance (2000–2011), enjoys friendly relations with and access to Putin (Hill & Gaddy, 2013, p. 249). Specifically in the area of economic policy Putin has on three occasions commissioned major policy reviews from outside sources: the so-called Gref Program as he first assumed the presidency; the 'Strategy-2020' programme in 2013; and the programme currently being developed under Kudrin's direction. The last is interesting because it is supposed to generate proposals jointly developed by Kudrin's fiscally conservative and anti-statist liberals on the one hand and the far more statist and stimulus-oriented members of the Stolypin Club on the other (Papchenkova & Prokopenko, 2016). Putin has also instituted in recent years a complex and highly bureaucratic process of strategic planning, which is supposed to closely tie economic policy making to strategic national goals (Cooper, n.d.; Monaghan, 2013, 2014).

Whatever use he makes of these various inputs, his core vision since coming to power and ever more assertively as he has retained it, is to gain for Russia the status of a great power, an autonomous actor controlling its destiny politically and economically at home and vigorously pursuing its interests on the world stage.

Such a vision requires most obviously a powerful military, supported by a well-resourced defence industry. That was not something that Putin was able to pursue with great vigour when he first came to power, but as he gained access to substantial financial resources – as oil prices rose and he asserted the state's control over the resulting revenues – the strength of the security apparatus, above all the military, became a major budget priority.

Putin's vision was never, however, limited to guns. He has always given considerable priority to butter, displaying particular solicitude for those sections of the population that rely on the state for their livelihood and therefore are his core electorate, specifically pensioners and *biudzhetniki*, that is, those who work for the state. They were a particular focus of the May decrees, the full implementation of which remains as a key priority. Major increases in pensions and subsequent full indexation were matters of pride. However recent economic difficulties have forced some retreat, including partial indexation of pensions in 2016 and allowing onto the agenda the principle of means testing (*adresnost'*) (kremlin.ru/events/president/52978; kremlin.ru/events/president/news/53045).

Through most of the decade and a half he has been in power Putin has calculated that the best way of achieving his major goals – a powerful defence capacity and an adequately well-off population – is control on the country's natural resources, above all oil and gas. He restored the state's control over those strategic resources, through the Yukos Affair and strategic investment legislation, then taxed the revenues earned from their sale at a level high enough to fund his security and social goals but without, as he once put it, 'killing the Golden Goose' (Vladimir Putin o nalogooblozhenii, 2008). The energy strategy also required a relative openness to foreign financing and technology imports, both to maintain output in mature fields and to open extremely challenging new deposits.[6]

Despite the scale of his ambitions and the riches that Russia's oil and gas have provided over his period in power, Putin has maintained a serious commitment to budget balance and fiscal discipline. Both to ensure Russia's sovereign independence from foreign financial markets and to protect the living standards of his electorate from inflation, he paid off Russia's sovereign debt as soon as he was able and has been reluctant to increase it since. He has been equally reluctant to allow significant budget deficits, and even agreed to transfer a significant proportion of Russia's resource export revenues to sovereign wealth funds (Fortescue, 2010).

Those two policy positions – reliance on hydrocarbon exports and a commitment to fiscal discipline – have always been challenged by those who insist that the economy must be diversified away from reliance on resource exports and that money has to be made available through more relaxed fiscal and monetary policy to pay for it. The more 'liberal' of those holding to that policy orientation have been called the 'modernisers', particularly when Medvedev tried to champion the approach during his presidency. They have focused their strategy on providing funding for infrastructure and the development of human capital. The Ministry of Economic Development (MED) has been a consistent advocate of such an approach. A more radical approach has come from those wanting much more expansive government spending directly on industry. At the risk of over-emphasising a single organisation, we will call those proposing such an approach the Stolypin Club, since it is indeed one of its key advocates. Putin has always been careful to support the so-called 'real economy', including its non-competitive parts, to the degree needed to ensure a functional defence industry and social stability.[7] However he has done so within the boundaries of fiscal responsibility and never to the satisfaction of either the modernisers or the Stolypin Club.

Since his return to the presidency Putin's adherence to his positions has been challenged not just by those with a policy alternative but also by circumstances. In the early stages of his third presidency it appeared that the apparent rebound from the crisis of 2008 was set to continue in the long term, meaning an economy awash in hydrocarbon earnings. This encouraged the modernisers to proclaim with a loud voice that the money should be spent on development, not salted away in reserve funds. Putin largely resisted the pressure. Thus he agreed with the Ministry of Finance (MF), against considerable opposition, that the so-called 'budget rule' be reinstated after its Global Financial Crisis (GFC)-induced suspension (Visloguzov, 2012). It was the budget rule that formed the basis of the controversial reserve funds, by requiring that a certain percentage of hydrocarbon revenues be set aside in them.

The post-GFC rebound turned out to be short-lived and even as oil prices climbed growth stagnated. This strengthened the modernisers in their view that the old model was broken, and that reserves had to be spent on growth-inducing infrastructure before it was too late. Putin showed signs of giving in to such pressures. *Moscow Times* wrote in May 2013 that 'Putin, who has long sat on the fence between the two camps, is now prodding the government towards more fiscal and monetary stimulus to shore up growth in the short term' (Putin can't blame, 2013). Thus his approval of the use of money from one of the reserve funds, the Fund for National Development, for infrastructure projects (Fortescue, 2016, p. 435). However, the insistence that such expenditure not be at the expense of a significant budget deficit was maintained, as can be seen in the quotation from his 2014 Address above.

With the arrival of sanctions and falling oil prices stagnation became recession and crisis, and to the cries of the modernisers were added the shouts of the supporters of radical stimulus. Putin came under strong pressure to run down reserves, loosen monetary policy and increase debt, in order to support and stimulate the 'real economy'. However, if anything these challenging circumstances reinforced his commitment to fiscal rectitude. In order to limit the size of the deficit even in crisis circumstances, he was prepared to accept cutbacks in his priority areas, with defence and the social sector having to give some ground. Having said that, he has allowed the budget deficit to expand in the last year or so, including significantly beyond the originally planned level in 2016,[8] and if we were being highly Kremlinogical we might suggest that he was much more restrained in his statements on the importance of macroeconomic stability in his 2016 Address than previously (kremlin.ru/events/president/news/53379).

If the commitment to fiscal rectitude has not been abandoned, or at least not entirely, has he shifted away from his reliance on the hydrocarbon export model? Undoubtedly he is aware of the threat to the energy model posed by what could be persistently lower oil prices. He continues to insist on high growth targets – higher than the average global growth rate – despite persistent forecasts that that will be difficult to attain.[9] As already mentioned he brought the Stolypin Club into the process of developing a new growth-oriented economic policy programme, albeit under the control of Aleksei Kudrin. In his 2016 Address he called for what seems to be yet another economic programme, to be drawn up by the end of May 2017, with the participation of the Chamber of Trade and Commerce and other business organisations and with the specific goal of achieving a growth rate above the global average by the end of 2019 (the end of the next budget cycle) (kremlin.ru/acts/assignments/orders/53425).[10] He talks of the defence industry sector as a 'locomotive' for growth and source of high-tech civilian output, while he is a vigorous proponent of import substitution with all the 'industry policy' expenditure it implies. But there is still something unconvincing about his commitment. The political and economic might of the oil and gas sector in Putin's

Russia is constantly demonstrated, and one is inclined to agree with Oleg V'iugin (2014) that the model has not essentially changed.

The budget process

Driven by the broad policy orientations just outlined, Putin sets budget parameters, with varying degrees of precision. After that it is the task of the government to develop a budget within those parameters. There are reasons why the process is not straightforward. Firstly, there is the obvious point that the budget process is largely about recipients of government revenues bidding in what is always likely to be a competitive way for budget allocations. Then, there are differences of opinion within the government's financial–economic block as to how a budget within the parameters is best achieved. Often the differences might appear to be technical, but they are rarely without some element of ideological belief and intra-agency competition (Butrin, 2016a). The differences become much sharper if the parameters appear to be mutually incompatible, something which arguably is becoming a genuine possibility if not existing reality.

Since 2006 the budget has been prepared on a three-year cycle, with a return to a one-year cycle as a one-off in the crisis circumstances of 2008 and 2015. Even with the three-year cycle, the budget is worded, to take the current budget as an example, 'for 2017 and the plan period 2018 and 2019'. A budget is prepared annually, as legislation which goes through the parliament and is signed into law by the president.[11] This means that later changes have to be passed by the parliament as amendments to the Budget Law. The 2016 Budget went through a fraught amendment process in October of that year (Butrin & Rotenberger, 2016).

The drawing up of the budget begins with MED preparing a rough draft of its Forecast of Socio-Economic Development for the relevant budget period. In 2016 the first version appeared in early March, it was delivered to the government in mid-April, and was presented to cabinet on 21 April. The Forecast contains the basic economic data – the most important being oil price, rate of inflation and capital flows – on the basis of which the Ministry of Finance calculates budget revenues (which is not to suggest that the Ministry of Finance does not develop its own figures). The Forecast is always presented in the form of several scenarios, which have gone by different names year by year, including 'basic' (the most 'conservative' or pessimistic), 'moderately optimistic', 'optimistic' and 'goal-oriented' (*tselevoi*). Each scenario contains a forecast growth rate. For scenarios other than the goal-oriented the settings are forecast and then an achievable growth rate calculated from them. The goal-oriented scenario is explicitly based on a desired growth rate, with the other settings that would be needed to meet it then calculated. It has in the past been presented for illustrative purposes only, since the set growth rate is usually acknowledged as unrealistic. However in current circumstances, with the growth rate becoming a matter of major policy concern, things are somewhat fluid. In the past the government used the 'moderately optimistic' scenario as the basis for budget formation. However, from 2013 the 'basic' scenario has been used, in recognition of the extreme risks in the global and domestic economy. That is a sign of Putin in cautious mode, allowing the Ministry of Finance (MF) to have its head. However such a scenario produces for the current budget period very low growth rates throughout, at a time when Putin has demanded a growth rate above the global average (at times interpreted to be around 4%) to be achieved by 2019. That is the growth rate in the goal-oriented forecast (Butrin, 2016c). It appears that the contradiction will be left unresolved for 2017, the first year of the budget. The expectation presumably is that for the following year – with a sense that the economic situation is already improving better than predicted in the pessimistic 'basic' scenario – a more optimistic forecast will be provided.

As should already be clear, the government's approval of the Forecast is a fraught process, with MF habitually criticising the numbers going into it as excessively optimistic and insisting on their moderation. While the adoption of the Forecast by the government is an early part of the budget process, in practice – and particularly when economic circumstances are volatile – it is revised throughout. In the preparation of the 2017–2019 budget, with the issue of growth rates lurking in the background, there was a particularly sharp public struggle between MF and the Central Bank, on the one hand, and MED on the other, with it being claimed that the former two subverted the forecasting process by insisting that settings be changed – and getting directives from the prime minister to get their way – in order to allow the budget figures to add up, regardless of what the Ministry of Economics might have thought was likely to happen. A major point of contention was the forecast inflation rate (Prokopenko, 2016a).

Once a preliminary Forecast has been accepted, MF sets what it sees as the likely distribution of funds among the various sectors of the economy. The prime minister undertakes a hectic series of 'sectoral' meetings (*soveshchaniia*) with the key bidders for government expenditures, grouped into six broad categories, plus a separate meeting for regional transfers. The only accounts we have of these meetings are Medvedev's brief introductory comments.[12] In most cases they are very general and uninformative. At one such meeting in 2016, that for science and sport, Medvedev noted that the president had directed that the spending on fundamental research be set at a percentage of GDP no lower than that in 2015 (which means a cut, since GDP has fallen), and that the May decrees set targets for pay in the sector. He went on that MF had sent ministries their funding limits, and that no doubt they had their own proposals for extra funding. He warned that any proposals for extra budgetary allocations were unlikely to be successful, but proposals for redistribution and, in extreme cases, the use of reserves could be considered (government.ru/news/23906). Although this was the only occasion on which a statement that there were items that had to be funded to a set level was put on the public record, it is probably a reasonable outline of the way the meetings generally go – the submission of bids, sometimes with specific presidential commitments to back them up, in the context of a broad outline of what funding is likely to be available.

In 2016, after the sectoral meetings had been completed (the first was on 20 July, the last 6 September), Medvedev convened a meeting on 21 September

> since we have completed all the basic sectoral meetings and arrived at decisions on most issues. Now we approach the next key point on the road – the basic parameters of the forecast of the country's socio-economic development, so that on its basis we can arrive at a balance between revenues and expenditure in the federal budget (government.ru/news/24604/).

This is an odd way of putting it, since the Forecast had already been approved by cabinet, but it is an indication of the extent to which so much is still up for grabs.

The preparatory outlines of the budget are then put together as the so-called Basic Directions of Budgetary Policy (*Osnovnye napravleniia biudzhetnoi politiki*). MF has the lead responsibility for preparing it and other budget documents. It does so against the background of the preparation of a number of other Basic Directions for other components of economic policy, including the Basic Directions for Government Activity (the responsibility of MED), the Basic Directions for Tax Policy (MF), and the Basic Directions for Monetary and Credit Policy (the Central Bank). All these documents are a source of controversy and politico-administrative battles in their own right. There is not the space here to deal with them in any detail, although some comment on the Basic Directions for Government Activity is offered.

As its name suggests, the Basic Guidelines for Government Activity is an overarching document setting out the government's programme for the year. Generally it has not attracted a great deal of analytical attention and one suspects that it has been something of a compilation of sectoral wish-lists. However it occasionally hits the headlines as an instrument in budgetary struggles. When in 2006 then Prime Minister Fradkov was engaged in a bitter struggle with Minister of Finance Kudrin over budgetary spending, he directed MF to take the Basic Directions into account in drawing up the budget, something which Kudrin avoided doing, ultimately with Putin's support (Netreba, 2006). While he was prime minister, Putin used the document to insist on a tough budget (archive.premier.gov.ru/events/news/10586/). As crisis hit the economy in 2014–2015, revision of the Basic Directions for Government Activity was used as a way to get some longer-term thinking into the economic policy process after a long period of day-to-day fire fighting. The usual competing policy preferences of different agencies were brought to bear, with MED pushing for a new development model based on import substitution, with the appropriate relaxation of fiscal rules to fund it, while MF insisted on a commitment to a balanced budget by 2017 (Bazanova & Liutova, 2014; Visloguzov, 2015). The final document included the growth target that Putin had introduced in his 2014 Address, that is, not lower than the global average, as well as reductions in federal budget expenditure of up to 5% in 2016 and 2017 and a balanced budget by 2017. Overall this was seen as a victory for MF, even if we know with hindsight that those targets were well and truly missed. It is unclear whether the prominence of the Basic Directions for Government Activity in the cases mentioned was a response to unusual circumstances or a reflection of more fundamental changes driven by the implementation of strategic planning methodologies (Sapozhkov, 2015).

As the key budget planning document, the Basic Directions of Budget Policy are put together by MF in the form of an outline of revenues and expenditures. In draft form the document is considered in both government and presidential meetings (*soveshchaniia*), as well as meetings (*zasedaniia*) of the Government Commission for Budget Policy.[13] Once the document is approved by cabinet, MF begins work on putting together the full draft budget. It is considered in a number of *soveshchaniia* and once something like agreement has been reached, it is taken to the Government Commission for Budget Policy and then the cabinet.[14] Right up to the moment the budget is sent to the parliament there are arguments, negotiations and adjustments.

It will have been noted by the careful reader that all the agencies and individuals mentioned in this brief account of the budget process have been from within the government. Does Putin have any involvement in the process, or is his participation limited to setting strategic priorities and relying on the government to form a budget according to them? In providing a detailed account of the budget process as it existed early in Putin's first presidency, Iwasaki (2002) does not mention the president's involvement beyond setting parameters in the Budget Address. Is that still the case today?

Putin and the process

When Putin returned to the presidency in 2012 it looked as if he was going to increase the president's involvement in operational policy making by setting up a 'second government' in the Presidential Administration (PA) (Fortescue, 2016, p. 8). A number of ministers from the government he had chaired as prime minister transferred to the PA as his assistants (*pomoshchniki*). Generally the experiment, if that was what it was intended to be, did not work. The assistants either drifted away or remained in what could only be described as sinecures. Economic policy could well be the exception. Putin's first assistant in this area was Elvira Nabiullina, who had served in his government as Minister for Economic Development. She is a standard and reasonably strict 'liberal', in the sense of an adherent to fiscal discipline and monetary restraint (although not so much so that as minister she did not present the ministry's standard growth-oriented line) (Kuvshinova & Kaz'min, 2009). As Putin's assistant it is said that she signed off on any significant economic decisions and zealously pursued the implementation of the May decrees (Proskurnina, Pis'mennaia, & Tovkailo, 2013). Although that required ensuring that large sums of money were spent, there is no reason to believe that she was any less committed than Putin to ensuring that the expenditure was within the limits of a nearly balanced budget.

She did not remain in the position very long, moving to head the Central Bank in 2013, where she became a favourite hate figure for the proponents of growth for her vigorous use of high interest rates. She was replaced as assistant by Andrei Belousov, who had been her replacement as Minister for Economics. His previous career included deputy Minister of Economic Development from 2006 and director of the Economics and Finance Department of the central government apparatus from 2008 (that is, while Putin was prime minister). He has always championed strong pro-modernisation and growth policies.[15] While Minister for Economic Development he was unusual in the degree to which he publicly stressed the importance of a growing defence budget.[16]

He is an active assistant, and indeed has appeared as a participant in government meetings, a significant departure from tradition and protocol. The first time was in June 2013, immediately after his appointment to the assistant position, when he attended and was recorded as a member of the Government Commission on Budget Policy in the published list of participants (http://government.ru/news/2590/).[17] That was a status that Nabiullina had never enjoyed. It was not until September 2014 that he was listed as attending a government *soveshchanie* in his capacity as Putin's assistant. That first one was chaired by Medvedev to discuss monetary-credit policy. No official list of participants was published, but the newspaper *Kommersant* provided a credible list which included Belousov (Butrin, 2014b). Later that year he was included in the official list of participants of a Medvedev-chaired *soveshchanie* on the economic crisis (government.ru/news/16145/). From then on Belousov was usually included if a list was published, although it is interesting to note that of the seven sectoral meetings mentioned above, he attended only three (those dealing with science and sport, housing services and construction, and agriculture and fishing).[18] On one occasion, a June 2016 meeting to discuss the basic parameters of the 2017–2019 budget, Belousov was not present, but Vladimir Simonenko, head of the presidential administration's Expert Division, was, presumably as a replacement (government.ru/news/23421).

What policy line does Belousov pursue in these forums? The proceedings are not published, so we do not know what he says. His past policy positions, with a strong emphasis on state spending to promote economic growth, appear to be somewhat at odds with Putin's, who has generally supported MF's line. Nevertheless, he has continued to express such views. Thus, it is said, he recommended to Putin that the Stolypin Club be included in the development of Kudrin's economic development programme (Papchenkova & Prokopenko, 2016). As already suggested, there are signs of Putin becoming more receptive to an 'industry policy' approach since Belousov has been in influential positions, although the author has already expressed doubts as to how committed the president is. On defence spending they are definitely on the same wavelength.

Belousov's career suggests that Putin values his policy advice – he was transferred to his apparatus when Putin became prime minister, and then after a brief hiatus to the presidential apparatus when Putin returned to the Kremlin. Even if they do not share views on everything, Putin clearly appreciates having near him someone with definite views that he is not afraid to express, and with good links throughout the economics community and considerable experience of economic policy making.

Once it became clear that the 'second government' approach, with the partial exception of the economics assistant, had not gained traction, Putin turned to what could be called the 'second prime minister' approach. That is, Putin became more directly involved personally in government policy processes, including budget formation.

Firstly, he began meeting on a regular, collective basis with members of the government. The meetings take place fortnightly (with for some reason in 2016 a gap from late April to early June). They are used to discuss the whole range of policy issues, including the budget.[19]

Secondly, he began presiding over *soveshchaniia* dealing with economic policy issues. This was not new – it was something that Medvedev also did as president.[20] In opening one such meeting in November 2016 Putin referred to 'us meeting regularly in such a format, with the leadership of the government, the Central Bank, and the [presidential] administration' (kremlin.ru/events/president/news/53237). A typical example took place in September 2012, to consider the draft budget (news.kremlin.ru/news/16493).

Putin stressed the need for budget balance and the fight against inflation, but also that resources must be found for the implementation of the May decrees. Indeed he declared that the draft budget MF had delivered to the government the day before was unacceptable in its current form, because it did not provide adequate resources for the decrees (Ivakhnik, 2012). Another example is a meeting on 16 September 2013. The official record includes only Putin's opening remarks (kremlin.ru/events/president/news/17342). Newspaper accounts suggested that as ever MF and MED presented their competing views (Kuvshinova, 2013; Liutova, 2013). As ever Putin tried to hedge. He seemed to leave the question of whether there should be demand stimulus open for debate, although he made clear that the budget rule had to be maintained. He supported the idea of investment in infrastructure. As another example, a newspaper report in September 2014 claimed that the usual warring ministries were able to reach agreement on MED's latest Forecast and the Central Bank's Basic Directions of Monetary-Credit Policy only after a Putin *soveshchanie* with members of the government held on 10 September 2014 (Butrin, 2014a). In the account of the meeting on the presidential website Putin says that he had discussed the issues with unnamed colleagues for four hours the previous day. No discussion or outcomes are recorded (kremlin.ru/events/president/news/46592). It was then reported in the press that a subsequent meeting was held to resolve remaining differences on 17 September (Kuvshinova, Tovkailo, & Liutova, 2014). That meeting was officially reported on the presidential website, although with no details and no list of participants (news/kremlin.ru/news/46635). Two years later, another Putin *soveshchaniia* drew a line of sorts under similar disagreements within the financial–economic block over budget targets, including ruling in favour of MF and the Central Bank in their insistence that MED reduce the expected level of inflation in its Forecast to 4% (kremlin.ru/events/president/news/52978).[21]

The third form of Putin's personal involvement in budget matters is one-on-one meetings between Putin and Medvedev, deputy prime ministers and ministers. When in October 2015 Medvedev raised in the Government Commission on Budget Policy the sensitive issue of only partially indexing pensions and the salaries of state employees (including in the military), he noted that he had discussed the matter with Putin (government.ru/news/20002/). In opening the series of sectoral meetings referred to above Medvedev noted that he had discussed the budget with Putin the previous day – the official report of that meeting is very *pro forma* as far as the budget was concerned (Putin did express concern about the strengthening of the ruble) (kremlin.ru/events/president/news/52544; government.ru/news/23906/).[22] In their meetings with Putin, Uliukaev and his predecessor as Minister for Economic Development Belousov used the opportunity to press their policy priorities (news.kremlin.ru/news/16526; news.kremlin.ru/news/18401). An interesting meeting took place between Putin not long after he had returned to the presidency with the newly appointed Minister of Finance Siluanov. It was unusual because Putin turned the conversation to the place of defence spending in budget planning, saying:

> I know that you [the Ministry of Finance] and the Ministry of Defence have found relatively flexible instruments for deciding all tasks confronting us in this sphere. There might be some useful things that can be done regarding the readiness or lack of readiness of industry to fulfil these tasks. Industry needs reequipping. And for that we have identified substantial resources. But for us to feel confident – I want, and I emphasise that I want you [Siluanov personally] and other colleagues to know …,

and he goes on to stress his commitment to fiscal discipline (news.kremlin.ru/news/16276).[23]

Putin is clearly involved in budget formation in a far more direct and operational way than setting strategy and parameters in his Address and other forums. He, or his economic assistant, ensures that his policy priorities are included in the budget, and he resolves policy disputes within the government. Although he is often as keen to occupy the middle ground as in other policy areas, there is no sign of the irritation at or resistance to the expectations placed on him as a resolver of conflict within the government that we see in other policy areas (Fortescue, 2016, pp. 445–446). Neither do we find the undermining of *soglasovanie* procedures that we find in other policy areas. The budget process is still highly structured and relatively orderly. There is insufficient evidence to suggest that Putin's *ruchnoe upravlenie* is producing 'policy irresponsibility' in this area.

Conclusion

Budget formation entails a lot of 'technocratic' activity within the government, with all the debate and conflict between agencies that that phrase hides. This has contributed to if not caused a steady drawing out of the process, as deadlines are extended while agencies fight and Medvedev is unable to force a conclusion. This has occurred to the degree that Putin has had to intervene to a significant degree. As just suggested, there is not the evidence to suggest that his *ruchnoe upravlenie* has brought about 'policy irresponsibility'. This is probably because his commitment to budget issues has been genuine, not imposed, and that while as always trying to hedge he has also been reasonably consistent in his expectations. Government actors therefore have some confidence in their sense of where they stand and that their views have standing, even if they are not always accepted.

One's ultimate evaluation depends on one's general view of the adequacy or otherwise of Russian economic policy. If one is of the view that Russian economic and budget policy has been well-managed – if one believes that it is a policy that has led to considerable growth to the benefit of the Russian population and the country's place in the world, and that it has weathered two major crises without the catastrophic collapse many predicted – then Putin can take much of the credit. He has largely got the balance right between taxing and allowing the development of the resource sector, and he has kept the lid on inflation while keeping the major claimants on state revenues happy.

If one is of the view that Russian economic and budget policy has been a failure – if one believes that massive resource revenues have been squandered without any serious effort to diversify the economy or to drag it out of stagnation, even before recklessly self-imposed sanctions made things much more difficult – then Putin is also responsible.

Even those with a generally positive view of Russian economic management are likely to agree that the pressures on the budget are increasing. Is the model described here – of Putin being directly involved in the budget process to the degree needed to enforce his priorities but not to such a degree as to induce 'policy irresponsibility' – resilient enough to withstand such pressures?

There are certainly some signs of financial pressures impacting the budget process. There is the introduction of a new instrument to ensure the funding of priority areas, the 'project office';[24] the unusual appearance of tax arrangements in the budget process in 2016 (usually tax arrangements are negotiated separately and taken as a given in the budget process; the major taxpayers are not represented in a process which is about allocating expenditures not collecting revenues) (Butrin, 2016b; kremlin.ru/events/president/news/52978);[25] the use of government directives to force the economic agencies to adopt particular budget settings and targets, particularly MED to include specific targets in its forecasts; Putin's commitment to a rate of growth that cannot be achieved under accepted official forecasts; and small signs of the breakdown of *soglasovanie* procedures that has created such havoc in other policy-making areas (Prokopenko, 2016b).

These are all interesting developments that deserve detailed attention. Here we limit ourselves to some very cursory comments: that it is hard to see how the project office approach will have a major impact on budget formation; perhaps partly because the main taxpayers are not represented, the tax discussions have not gone far; we should not exaggerate how much the use of directives differs from past practice in ensuring forecasts and budget planning documents comply with political and policy imperatives through hard bargaining; the growth issue has been deliberately left hanging while all parameters are so volatile; and the budget process is still highly regimented and 'consultative', with all participants playing a highly engaged role.

None of this is to say that the budget process remains sufficiently robust to endure serious pressures on the revenue side and the resultant intensification of the struggle for funding on the expenditure side. If truly hard choices have to be made between guns, butter and development, those choices will be made by Putin in a way which will inevitably have significant implications for the process of forming the budget. Players who are used to compromise and processes that encourage it will find that the room for compromise has shrunk to nothing, which could well involve losing players being effectively excluded from the process. But for the moment all participants are able to contribute their specific expertise and policy positions. Putin shows every sign of being aware of the implications of the policy options which are available and of taking them into account.

Notes

1. In Russian parlance what we would call the cabinet is also known as the 'government'. The Western usage is preferred here.
2. For suggestions that it has, see Aptekar' and Sinitsyn (2015), Monaghan (2013, p. 1232), and Papchenkova and Liutova (2015).
3. Article 114.1(a): The government draws up and presents the federal budget to the State Duma, and secures its implementation.
4. On the significance of this, see Iwasaki (2002, p. 308).
5. On those thoughts and experiences, see Hill and Gaddy (2013).
6. Nigel Gould-Davies (2016) uses the phrase 'sovereign globalisation' to describe the simultaneous determination to control strategic resources while being sufficiently open to the world to exploit them.
7. His response to the threat of enterprise closures at Pikalevo in 2009 illustrates the commitment to the latter (Fortescue, 2009).
8. The original figure in the 2016 budget was 3.1%. By the time the budget was formally amended in November 2016 it had reached 3.7%. At a meeting soon after Putin said: 'the budget deficit should be 3.7% – and that's where it is. True, there is the risk of a small increase. … Of course, there's nothing terrible if it gets to 3.8 or 3.9, but all the same we should strive to keep it within the boundaries of the [budget] law' (kremlin.ru/events/president/news/53237).
9. The MED draft Forecast to 2035, released in October 2016, sees growth 1.5 times lower than the global average well into the future (Kuvshinova & Prokopenko, 2016).
10. The Chamber of Trade and Industry is the successor body of the Soviet organisation of the same name. It has generally been seen as more 'conservative' than other business associations, and has not featured prominently in recent economic policy making.
11. The passage of the budget legislation through the Duma is the focus of Benjamin Noble's contribution to this special issue.
12. For a list of the meetings in 2016 for the 2017–2019 budget, with links to Medvedev's introductory comments and lists of participants, see government.ru/news/24604/.
13. As the language of a nation with a rich bureaucratic tradition, Russian has several words for 'meeting'. Two are used here. A *soveshchanie* is a meeting of a group of individuals, rather than of a formally constituted body. They might meet together regularly and in quite a routinised way, or the meetings might be one-offs in response to particular circumstances. A *zasedanie* is a meeting of a formally constituted body with an established membership.
14. The commission's full name is Government Commission for Budget Policy for the Coming Financial Year and Plan Period, that is, reflecting the planning cycle but also indicating that the Commission is not involved in long-term planning.
15. For examples from each stage of his career, see Petrachkova (2006), Kuvshinova (2011), and finally, Pis'mennaia, Tovkailo, and Kuvshinova (2012).
16. For examples, see Pis'mennaia et al. (2012) and government.ru/news/1715/.
17. The formal decree formalising his membership seems to have been issued only in August 2013 (government.ru/info/2620/).
18. The presidential administration was represented at the meeting on regional funding by presidential advisor Igor Levitin and that on natural resources and the environment by Vladimir Simonenko, head of the presidential administration's Expert Division. It had no representation at the rest.

19. For one example of many, see kremlin.ru/events/president/news/50185. One this occasion Medvedev was absent. There appears to be no rule regarding the presence or absence of the prime minister at these meetings.
20. For examples of President Medvedev's *soveshchaniia* specifically on budget matters, see news.kremlin.ru/news/12575 and news.kremlin.ru/transcripts/12769. As with Putin's meetings with members of the government, there appears to be no rule as to whether the prime minister attends these meetings. Under both presidents the practice has varied.
21. One newspaper account of this disagreement refers to an earlier Putin *soveshchanie*, on 22 September (Butrin, 2016b). It is not reported on the Kremlin website.
22. Another meeting on the budget, held on 25 October, is reported in no less *pro forma* terms (kremlin.ru/events/president/news/53144).
23. Julian Cooper provides more detail on the involvement of the defence sector in the budget process in his contribution to this special issue.
24. The new presidential Commission for Strategic Development and Priority Projects, of which the operational arm is its presidium under the chairmanship of Medvedev, has responsibility for 11 priority areas, most of which could be seen as having a social element. Medvedev has stated that budget planning must be coordinated with the Commission (government.ru/news/23676/; government.ru/news/24873).
25. Representatives of the oil sector were unusually present at a September 2015 Putin *soveshchanie* on budget formation, clearly because the possibility of extracting extra tax from them to fill holes in the 2016 budget was discussed (kremlin.ru/events/president/news/50344).

Disclosure statement

No potential conflict of interest was reported by the author.

References

Aptekar', P., & Sinitsyn, S. (2015). Biudzhetnyi protsess kak komediia polozhenii [Budget process as sitcom]. *Vedomosti*, 22 September.

Bazanova, E., & Liutova, M. (2014). Medvedevu predlozhen plan [Medvedev offered a plan]. *Vedomosti*, 22 April.

Butrin, D. (2014a). Ne vremia dlia vol'shebnikov [Not the time for magicians]. *Kommersant*, 15 September.

Butrin, D. (2014b). Pereotsenka na neft' [Repricing oil]. *Kommersant*, 25 September.

Butrin, D. (2016a). Strukturnyi profitsit vsemu golova [Structural surplus is best of all]. *Kommersant*, 15 June.

Butrin, D. (2016b). 'Rastroenie nalichnosti' [Cash upset]. *Kommersant*, 29 September.

Butrin, D. (2016c). Rost pustili na samotek [Growth left to drift]. *Kommersant*, 12 October.

Butrin, D., & Rotenberger, I. (2016). Biudzhet voennykh garantii [A budget of military guarantees]. *Kommersant*, 4 October.

Cooper, J. (n.d). *Reviewing Russian strategic planning: the emergence of Strategy 2020, NDC Research Review*. Rome: NATO Defense College.

Fortescue, S. (2009). Putin in Pikalevo: PR or watershed? *Australian Slavonic and East European Studies., 23*, 19–38.

Fortescue, S. (2010). Russia's SWFs: controlled by a domestic agenda. In X. Yi-chong & G. Bahgat (Eds.), *The Political Economy of Sovereign Wealth Funds* (pp. 113–131). Palgrave: Basingstoke.

Fortescue, S. (2012). The policymaking process in Putin's prime ministership. In L. Jonson & S. White (Eds.), *Waiting for Reform under Putin and Medvedev* (pp. 119–139). Palgrave: Basingstoke.

Fortescue, S. (2016). Russia's 'turn to the East': a study in policy making'. *Post-Soviet Affairs., 32*, 423–454.

Fortescue, S. (2017). Russia's security-related decision-making: The case of Crimea, In M. Steven Fish, G. Gill, M. Petrovic (eds), *A quarter century of post-communism assessed* (pp. 295–318). Basingstoke: Palgrave.

Gould-Davies, N. (2016). *Russia's sovereign globalization: Rise, fall and future*. London: Chatham House Research Paper.
Hill, F., & Gaddy, C. G. (2013). *Mr. Putin. operative in the Kremlin*. Washington DC: Brookings Institution Press.
Ivakhnik, A. (2012). Putin nedovolen biudzhetom i pravitel'stvom [Putin unhappy with the budget and the government]. *Politcom.ru*, 19 September, Retrieved from politcom.ru/14543.html.
Iwasaki, I. (2002). the state budget compilation process in Russia: Institutional framework and practice. *Post-Communist Economies., 14*, 301–319.
Kuvshinova, O. (2011). V tselom: nuzhen novyi motor [To sum up: a new motor is needed], *Vedomosti*, 31 May.
Kuvshinova, O. (2013). Sproc na rost [Demand for growth], *Vedomosti*, 17 January.
Kuvshinova, O., & Kaz'min, D. (2009). Nuzhny piat' let [Five years are needed], *Vedomosti*, 25 March.
Kuvshinova, O., & Prokopenko, A. (2016). Minekonomrazvitiia prognoziruet eshche 20 let stagnatsii [Ministry of Economic Development predicts another 20 years of stagnation], *Vedomosti*, 20 October.
Kuvshinova, O., Tovkailo, M., Liutova, M. (2014). Mobilizatsionnyi biudzhet [Mobilisational budget], *Vedomosti*, 17 September.
Liutova, M. (2013). Putin posovetoval ne uvlekat'sia stimulirovaniem potrebitel'skogo sprosa [Putin advises not to get caught up in stimulating consumer demand], *Vedomosti*, 16 January.
Monaghan, A. (2013). Putin's Russia: shaping a grand strategy? *International Affairs., 89*, 1221–1236.
Monaghan, A. (2014). Defibrillating the Vertikal?. *Putin and Russian Grand Strategy*. Research Paper. London: Chatham House.
Netreba, P. (2006). Minfin otstoial biudzhet-2007 ot vsekh, krome prezidenta [Minfin defended the budget against everyone except the president]. *Kommersant*, 19 June.
Papchenkova, M., & Liutova, M. (2015). Pravitel'stvo pri pravitel'stve [The government under the government]. *Vedomosti*, 16 February.
Papchenkova, M., & Prokopenko, A. (2016). Putin poruchil razrabotat' al'ternativu kontseptsii Alekseia Kudrina [Putin directive that an alternative concept to Aleksei Kudrin's be developed]. *Vedomosti*, 25 July.
Petrachkova, A. (2006). Kak delit' biudzhet [How to divide up the budget]. *Vedomosti*, 26 October.
Pis'mennaia, E., Tovkailo, M., Kuvshinova, O. (2012). 'Vse trebuet deneg', - Andrei Belousov, ministr ekonomicheskogo razvitiia ['Everyone wants money' – Andrei Belousov, Minister of Economic Development]. *Vedomosti*, 6 December.
Prokopenko, A. (2016a). Minekonomrazvitiia skorrektiruet prognoz radi biudzheta [Ministry of Economic Development corrects its forecast for the sake of the budget]. *Vedomosti*, 2 October.
Prokopenko, A. (2016b). Novye pravila biudzheta [New budget rules]. *Vedomosti*, 19 October.
Proskurnina, O., Pis'mennaia, E., & Tovkailo, M. (2013). Ona tikho skazala 'da' [She quietly said 'yes']. *Vedomosti*, 14 March.
Putin can't blame global ills for economic crunch. (2013). *Moscow Times*, 13 May.
Sapozhkov, O. (2015). Napravleniia ne mogut bez pravil [Directions can't be without rules]. *Kommersant*, 14 August.
Stanovaia, T. (2014). Poslanie prezidenta: ozhidanie i real'nost' [The president's Address: expectation and reality]. *Politcom.ru*, 8 December, Retrieved frompolitcom.ru/18387.html.
V'iugin, O. (2014). Ekonomicheskii rost: novaia model' rosta vygliadit kak usilennaia staraia [Economic growth: the new growth model looks like the old one reinforced]. *Vedomosti*, 2 July.
Visloguzov, V. (2012). Minfin otstoial svoi dva protsenta [Minfin defended its two percent]. *Kommersant*, 17 December.
Visloguzov, V. (2015). Biudzhet szhatiiu ne poddaetsia [Budget not giving in to tightening]. *Kommersant*, 3 March.
Vladimir Putin o nalogooblozhenii neftianykh kompanii [Vladmir Putin on taxation of oil companies]. (2008). *Kommersant*, 12 May.

Index

For Product Safety Concerns and Information please contact our EU
representative GPSR@taylorandfrancis.com
Taylor & Francis Verlag GmbH, Kaufingerstraße 24, 80331 München, Germany

www.ingramcontent.com/pod-product-compliance
Ingram Content Group UK Ltd.
Pitfield, Milton Keynes, MK11 3LW, UK
UKHW050753180926
475701UK00007B/1027